Counselling skills
FOR TEACHERS

Counselling skills
FOR TEACHERS
Talking matters

Gail King

Open University Press
Buckingham · Philadelphia

Open University Press
Celtic Court
22 Ballmoor
Buckingham
MK18 1XW

e-mail: enquiries@openup.co.uk
world wide web: http://www.openup.co.uk

and
325 Chestnut Street
Philadelphia, PA 19106, USA

First Published 1999

A catalogue record of this book is available from the British Library

ISBN   0335 20001X (hb)   0335 200001 (pb)

Library of Congress Cataloging-in-Publication Data
King, Gail, 1949–
    Counselling skills for teachers / Gail King.
        p.   cm.
    Includes bibliographical references (p.) and index.
    ISBN 0-335-20001-X (hard). – ISBN 0-335-20000-1 (pbk.)
    1. Teacher participation in educational counseling – Great Britain.
2. Counseling in secondary education – Great Britain.   3. Pastoral
counseling – Great Britain.   I. Title.
LB1620.53.G7K56   1999
373.14'046–dc21   99-13283
                                                                              CIP

Typeset by Graphicraft Limited, Hong Kong

Printed and bound in Great Britain by
Marston Book Services Limited, Oxford

This book is dedicated to all the students with whom I have worked. By allowing me to hear their stories I have learned so much. My life has been richer for the experience.

Contents

Preface

When I was asked by Michael Jacobs to write this book my immediate response was one of pleasure. I had been working as a school counsellor for eight years and felt a book would make a splendid tribute to all the students that I had worked with during those years. I had also presented a number of counselling skills workshops for PGCE (Postgraduate Certificate of Education) students and always felt somewhat frustrated that I could not recommend a book which both described the counselling skills a secondary school teacher could use in her pastoral work with students and included some guidance about the practical aspects of using those skills in a school.

However, after the initial delight, I then had to face the challenge of trying to combine these two elements in one text. One of my difficulties was to examine and explain the concepts that I took for granted as a counsellor in a way that is relevant and useful for a teacher. I hope I have been successful.

Having described the various counselling skills, I point out that the skills need to be practised. Space does not allow me to include exercises and so the reader is recommended to read Michael Jacobs's book, *Swift to Hear*, which contains useful exercises. Throughout the text I have referred to the teacher as 'she'. This has been for the sake of simplicity. The pronoun 'he' could have been used equally well.

While I have also outlined some of the potential problems

and pitfalls I hope I have always managed to be positive. Much of the pastoral work done by teachers is immensely valuable. I can easily remember the teachers in my own school life who encouraged, supported and simply believed in me. As an adolescent I experimented with painting, music and language but finally settled on language as the best way of communicating with and understanding another human being. However, words are complex. By dint of the richness of language there is also ambiguity and confusion. In counselling I seek to find words to express thoughts and feelings. At times the task is difficult but helping another person to express themselves is rewarding. The struggle is worthwhile.

I would like to thank various people who have helped, encouraged and supported me in writing this book. I would like to thank Michael Jacobs for recognizing the potential in me for this book. I have valued his help and encouragement not only when I trained as a psychotherapist but now, dare I say it, as a writer. I also thank Moira Walker who supervised much of my work as a school counsellor. Her support and her down to earth approach were invaluable. I would also like to thank Maureen Cruickshank who had the vision and foresight to create a counselling post for me in The Beauchamp College, Leicestershire. I have also appreciated and valued the support given by my teaching colleagues at the school. I came to value them as friends and gained a tremendous respect for them as teachers who not only put in many hours but also gave of themselves. In addition I would like to acknowledge the assistance of Peter Fearon and John Sharman at Kibworth High School, Leicestershire who gave their time to discuss pastoral concerns in a middle school. Needless to say it was from the school students themselves that I learned most of all.

My thanks also go to my close friends and immediate family who encouraged me and who did not give up on me when I shut myself away to write. I mention Mary who has always helped me to keep things in perspective, and Dorothy who has provided a safe place for me to work out my thoughts and feelings. I would also like to thank Kay Brutnall for her help with the typing, and Rob who has tried to teach me word processing skills. Besides those skills I have valued his patience and unstinting belief in me. Finally, and by no means least, I wish to thank my children, Ashley and Cerys, who despite minding that their mother was sometimes preoccupied or busy writing, nevertheless supported me both practically and emotionally. Their love and support made it possible.

Acknowledgements

I would like to thank the following organizations for granting permission to quote from their publications.

Children's Legal Centre – *Offering Children Confidentiality: Law and Guidance*
British Association for Counselling (BAC) – *Codes of Ethics and Practice Guidelines.*

BAC point out that the codes are revised from time to time and so the reader is advised to check with BAC that the code quoted is the current one.

Chapter 1

Counselling skills in secondary education

In order to understand more about the use of counselling skills and the current status of counselling in secondary education, it is helpful to consider a brief history of counselling and pastoral care in schools. In taking a historical perspective it is clear that while needs other than strictly educational ones have long since been identified as a significant part of schooling, there has been no agreement as to how those needs should be met or by whom. The argument has been further complicated by the lack of clarity surrounding the definition of counselling, its place in schools and whether or not counselling is compatible with the teacher's role.

The ideological roots of pastoral care can be said to have been in the late eighteenth and early nineteenth century in the work of reforming headmasters of public schools among whom were Thomas Arnold of Rugby and Edward Thring of Uppingham. Through them the idea was promoted that a teacher's responsibility to his pupil was greater than the training of the mind through the classics. Indeed it was Arnold who emphasized religious and moral principles first, gentlemanly conduct second, and intellectual ability third. Arnold's Rugby was the prototype public school that provided pastoral care by the vertical division of the school into houses.

After the introduction of the Education Act 1902 the newly established secondary schools were modelled on the house system of the public school. Later when some of the old charity schools were converted into state schools, the tradition of caring for pupils was incorporated into the general ethos of caring for the individual as well as providing an education. In the 1940s and 1950s there was growing concern for the individual in society and by the 1960s there were significant pieces of research which had great impact on social policy. These include Musgrove's (1976) research into the family; the Newsons' work on parent–child relationships (1963); Douglas's (1964) research on the home and the school as well as the Crowther Report (CACE 1959); the Newsom Report (1963) and the Plowden Report (CACE 1967). The consensus of opinion was that the personal needs of children were not being met.

With comprehensive reorganization in the 1960s the structure for caring within a school saw many complex and diverse systems including vertical house systems, horizontal systems of years and schools within schools. What became clear was that structure alone did not make for adequate care provision and attention then turned to the technique and process by which pastoral care was delivered. The task of defining pastoral care was further complicated by the difficulties in distinguishing between guidance, counselling and pastoral care.

Undoubtedly many of the principles and concepts of counselling, especially from the humanistic school, had a significant influence on thinking and policy during the 1960s, especially the writings of Carl Rogers, Leona Tyler and C. Gilbert Wrenn. Teachers, social workers and youth workers seized upon concepts such as non-directiveness, unconditional positive regard and genuineness, incorporating them into their work.

It was actually in 1963 that the relationship between counselling and schools was first officially discussed in Britain at a seminar held by the National Association for Mental Health (NAMH) under the chairmanship of Lord James of Rusholme. It was agreed that many children 'find the common problems of personal and social adjustment difficult or disturbing', and that there were 'demands which are not being effectively met'. It was concluded that 'a need exists which might be met by counsellors' (NAMH 1970: 1). In response to this perceived need the Universities of Keele and Reading offered counsellor training to teachers with five years' teaching experience. The emphasis on those courses was person-centred, based on Carl Rogers's work (see Further reading). Other courses were soon established in other parts of the country with the emphasis varying from the therapeutic to careers guidance. At first it looked as if eventually there would be a counsellor appointed in every school. School counselling was, as Bolger (1982: 61) states, 'a new force in education, a source of controversy, a source of inspiration, a source of theoretical understanding, a source of practical skills'.

However, the role was often ill-defined and badly understood. This may have been because the role was imported from America, and while there is a common language there are many cultural differences, not least of which is the emphasis on vocational guidance in American schools. Clearly there was also some resistance and ambivalence concerning the need for professional counsellors, and after the initial interest and growth in specialist courses and rise in counsellor posts in schools, there followed a decline. Other factors played a part, mainly economic, since head teachers were required to 'give up' a teacher to provide a counsellor.

In the 1970s several criticisms were being voiced. One critic was Richardson (1979) who argued that counselling in schools was incompatible with the 'real' task of the school, which he regarded as the cognitive development of children. However, despite the criticism Richardson's article was useful in that it highlighted fundamental issues, especially regarding the nature of counselling and what it is that is done in schools and by whom.

The situation had changed so that from having 351 counsellors in schools in Britain in 1977, by 1987 there were only 90 (Mabey and Sorenson 1995). This resulted partly from the severe cuts in education in which counsellors were seen as a luxury, but also because there was a new and growing emphasis on the need for counselling skills for all teachers. This was influenced by the work of Egan and the increased interest in the use of counselling skills in applied settings and personal and social educational programmes. The net result was that there was a greater emphasis on educational and vocational counselling and a move away from personal counselling.

Recently there has been a renewed interest in counselling on a one-to-one basis because, despite the relevance and usefulness of the personal and social education (PSE) or personal and social development (PSD) programmes, teachers have been finding that individual students still need personal responses. Teachers are being faced with problems in school for which they are inadequately trained, and students are not receiving the help they need. The emphasis now is on equipping teachers with basic counselling skills: not training them as counsellors or to work as counsellors, but helping teachers perform their 'pastoral' work more effectively, and enabling them to recognize problems which need referring on to a specialist or a specialist agency. It is recognized that teachers need training to assess the different levels of problems, so that they work within their level of competence, do not suffer undue stress as a result of the work, and do not harm students.

There has undoubtedly been a lot of confusion about what counselling is and what it is not, and what can be done in schools. These elements need to be clarified. First it will be helpful to look at the teacher's remit. Section 1 of the Education Reform Act 1988 states that schools have a statutory responsibility to develop a curriculum which 'promotes the spiritual, moral, cultural, mental and physical development of pupils at the school and of society; and prepares such pupils for the opportunities, responsibilities and experiences of adult life'. The welfare function is stressed alongside the educative function.

Ribbins and Best (1985: 22) offer a useful definition of this welfare or pastoral care element: 'Pastoral care has four inter-related dimensions (disciplinary/order, welfare/pastoral, academic/curricular; and administrative/organizational).' This definition addresses the complex role of the teacher and the potential for conflict between the dimensions, especially between welfare and disciplinary functions. This point is very important and is discussed later (see boundaries in Chapter 4).

As stated above some of the spiritual, moral, cultural, mental and physical needs can be met through the curriculum, but the overall ethos of the school can make a significant contribution. The interaction between the students, teachers and the system makes for effective schooling. As Rudduck *et al.* (1996: 1) state:

> whilst teachers are, for the most part supportive, stimulating and selfless in the hours they put in to help young

people, the conditions of learning that are common across secondary schools do not adequately take account of the social maturity of young people, nor of the tensions and pressures they feel as they struggle to reconcile the demands of their social and personal lives with the development of their identity as learners.

Each establishment needs to consider the ethos within the school and take steps to ensure it creates an environment in which students' collective and individual needs are met. To this end schools need to consider their policies relating to bullying; racial and sexual harassment; drugs; alcohol; smoking. Some problems need to be addressed at an individual level, but others also need to be dealt with in an educative way, through the curriculum (for example, bullying or harassment). It is through its formal PSE or PSD programme that a school can help promote a safe and healthy environment. In the PSD lesson a teacher can explore personal, moral and social issues through literature, exercises and discussion. Programmes are available suitable for each age group that raise awareness of issues and give practical support to the underlying ethos of the school.

However, despite attention being paid to this overall ethos, a school's policies and the effectiveness of its PSD programmes within each class, attention is still required to meet the individual's needs. It is this area that has been the subject of greatest confusion and argument. The question is how best to recognize and meet the individual's needs and by whom those needs should be met.

In the past commentators have argued that it is the teacher who is best placed to meet an individual student's needs. It is the teacher who is closest to the student in the school and knows the student better than does anyone else. It has been argued that the only person who can be continually effective is the teacher. This presumes intimate knowledge of the student and gives rise to the phrase 'every teacher a counselor' (Arbuckle 1950: 9). However, it is interesting to note that later (1965: 187) Arbuckle changed his position and stated, 'I was the first person to write a book using the term "teacher-counselor". Since then however it has become abundantly clear to me that the two simply do not go together.' He went on to say that 'the teacher is not a counselor or psychotherapist, either from the point of view of his education or his knowledge, and it is doubtful that his functions include becoming involved in a real counseling relationship with a child' (Arbuckle 1966: 158). Here Arbuckle draws attention to an extremely significant point regarding the relationship that exists between a counsellor and his client. Put simply, the point is that there is a different sort of relationship between a student and her teacher and a student and her counsellor. The major differences relate to confidentiality, boundaries and the contractual nature of the relationship (see professional boundaries and confidentiality in Chapters 4 and 6).

At the heart of the whole debate lies confusion about the nature of counselling, the nature of the therapeutic relationship, the aims of counselling and the significance and importance of boundaries. Patterson (1971: 87) acknowledges there is a common misunderstanding of what counselling is. He explains,

> If counselling were only a matter of giving information or advice, or solving another person's problems, the amount of information the counsellor had about the client might be important. However, counselling is a relationship in which the counsellor must understand the client as the latter sees himself and as he perceives the world; factual information is not necessary for this kind of understanding.

Some argument has focused on practical matters such as resources, time, training, or suitable office space; but of more fundamental importance is personal suitability and a proper understanding of the nature of counselling.

At this point it is useful to consider some definitions of counselling and distinguish between counselling and the use of counselling skills. Great confusion and misunderstanding have arisen over the years leading some people to think that anyone can counsel. Such claims are inaccurate. As Keppers (1956) noted, 'The fact that good teachers have always done counselling does not mean that all teachers have done good counselling.' Claims that anyone can counsel underestimate the counsellor's skills and undervalue her responsibilities.

Counselling definitions

Some early definitions of counselling tend to reflect the under-lying values in counselling stemming from its Judeo-Christian roots, or stress an advice-giving function. However, such definitions are either inadequate or inappropriate and perhaps more suited to lawyers who may be approached for 'good counsel'. Counsel-ling developed from psychoanalysis (Freud) and was first intro-duced as such to Britain in the 1950s via the National Marriage Guidance Council, now Relate.

Psychoanalysis and psychotherapy had been known about since the beginning of the twentieth century but it was the humanistic school of psychology and particularly the work and research of Carl Rogers that had a profound influence on the rise of the counselling movement (see Further reading). Alongside this person-centred approach was the influence of the Behaviourist School (Skinner (1953); Watson (1924)). Subsequently other theo-rists developed different models of therapy and added to the diversity of counselling.

Some definitions of counselling have focused on the process or what happens between the helper and the client. For example, Jones (1970: 10) suggests counselling is 'an enabling process, designed to help an individual come to terms with his life as it is and ultimately to grow to greater maturity through learning to take responsibility and to make decisions for him-self'. Or Williams (1973: 36) suggests, 'counselling is a process of sharing not only behaviour but experience, the creation of a relationship of such trust and confidence that the defensive walls we erect around ourselves are dismantled stone by stone'.

Some definitions have focused on the relationship between the helper and the client and the problem-solving nature of coun-selling. For example, the National Association for Mental Health (1970: paragraph 2.11) defines counselling as 'a relationship between two people, one needing an opportunity of talking over his problems, the other having the sensitivity and maturity thor-oughly to appreciate the uncertainties and conflicts involved, and having the necessary knowledge and skills to enable a solution or at least some accommodation to the difficulty to be reached'. Other definitions encompass the underlying values, the aims of counselling, the nature and process of the helping relationship.

Some definitions are too long and unwieldy to be helpful, but a very clear definition is provided by the British Association for Counselling (BAC). 'Counselling involves a deliberately undertaken contract with clearly agreed boundaries and commitment to privacy and confidentiality. It requires explicit and informed agreement' (BAC 1998: paragraph 3.2).

In the counselling literature the words 'counselling' and 'psychotherapy' are both used. Much debate flourishes regarding the use of the two terms. Some writers use the term interchangeably; others find the notion of a continuum of helping useful, with counselling at one end and psychotherapy at the other, while others regard psychotherapy as distinct from counselling and as being concerned with change to the personality. The BAC finds there is no generally accepted distinction between the two and so uses the term 'counselling'. For the purposes of this book the term counselling is preferred and where 'psychotherapy' is used this is only in direct quotations.

A second source of confusion relates to the difference between a counsellor and those who use counselling skills in the service of their main work, for example, nurse, teacher, social worker, tutor, line manager, personnel officer. BAC (1999: B) states that counselling skills are being used 'when there is an intentional use of specific interpersonal skills which reflects the values of counselling and the practitioner's primary role is enhanced without being changed and when the recipient perceives the practitioner as acting within their primary professional or/caring role which is not that of being a counsellor'.

A further distinction is made regarding aims. For the counsellor the aim is 'to facilitate the client's work in ways which respect the client's values, personal resources and capacity for choice within his or her cultural context' (BAC 1998: paragraph 3.1) whereas for the practitioner using counselling skills the aim is 'to serve the best interests of the client' (BAC 1999: B). There is some potential for conflict here. At times, the best interests of the client may be at variance with the demands of the teacher in her primary role. For example, a year head may have to tread a fine line between being a caring listener one day and being the person who dispenses discipline the next.

Another distinction is made relating to the scope of the work. For those using counselling skills as an adjunct to their main role, the purpose may be said to be 'to recognize feelings, thoughts and behaviours and, when appropriate, to explore them in greater depth' (BAC 1999: C.5) whereas the counsellor seeks 'to provide an opportunity for the client towards living in a way he or she experiences as more satisfying and resourceful' (BAC 1998: paragraph 3.1).

Underpinning the work, as both definitions make clear, is the need to respect clients, their values and their cultural context. The basic values of integrity, impartiality and respect are fundamental to all this type of work. Teachers and counsellors alike need to be aware of their own prejudices, biases and stereotyping and ensure that they maintain anti-discriminatory standards (see self-awareness in Chapter 4).

While counsellors and those using counselling skills hold the common values of integrity, impartiality and respect and also practise an anti-discriminatory approach, there are important areas of difference relating to confidentiality, responsibility, contracts, boundaries and the relationship itself. Of particular importance to the teacher is the issue of confidentiality. High standards are expected of both the counsellor and the teacher using counselling skills in order to create the trust which is so necessary in counselling work. To this end the conditions on which confidentiality is offered by the counsellor are made clear from the outset. For the teacher confidentiality needs to be 'consistent with their primary professional or work role. Any limits to confidentiality must be made explicit' (BAC 1999: C.3). Obviously this is vital when dealing with a student who is likely to disclose sexual or physical abuse, or who wishes to discuss contraception (see confidentiality in Chapter 6).

While there are other differences between the two BAC codes (that is the *Code of Ethics and Practice for Counsellors* (1998) and the *Code of Ethics and Practice Guidelines for Those Using Counselling Skills in their Work* (1999)), a final point needs to be made regarding competence and training. Both BAC codes make it clear that counsellors and practitioners using counselling skills need to work within the limits of their competence. The counsellor needs to monitor and develop her competence and she must have regular and ongoing supervision. By contrast, although the teacher needs to ensure her training in counselling skills is appropriate for the work she undertakes, the code relating to counselling skills only 'highly recommends' supervision.

Summary

Caring about the welfare of students, as well as their formal education, has been an important dimension of teaching for many years. The emphasis has shifted from pastoral care as being part of the teacher's responsibilities to the introduction of specialist counsellors and more recently to the recommendation that all teachers possess counselling skills. Given that many teachers are involved in pastoral care it is helpful for them to learn counselling skills so that they can carry out their pastoral work more effectively. In the next two chapters I describe some of the listening and responding skills that can be used in the helping process.

Chapter 2

Listening skills

Many introductory courses to counselling include a skills-based element that is often based on a micro-training model. The roots of micro-training lie in the micro-teaching programmes of the late 1960s in the USA. In these programmes teachers focused on a specific skill, practised it while conducting a small class for between five and 25 minutes, and then reviewed the skill with their supervisor. This method has been applied to counselling skills training programmes and has been found to be especially effective.

Micro-training is a model of instruction that breaks down complex human behaviour into discrete behavioural units and then teaches those units through instruction, practice, observation and feedback. The cycle is repeated until competency is reached in each unit. The micro-training model rests on behavioural foundations, with modelling as a significant factor. Despite this behavioural foundation many skills can be taught without an emphasis on any particular theoretical model, and so can be adapted to suit different helpers in different contexts, for example, nurses in a hospital or teachers in a school. It is however recognized by micro-training teachers that despite its very wide application there are some limitations especially because insufficient attention has been paid to cultural factors.

There is no standard classification of counselling skills or common vocabulary but some writers have attempted to classify the helping skills, for example, skills for understanding; skills for comfort and crisis utilization, and skills for positive action (Brammer 1976). Other writers have developed models that clearly set out the skills required for each stage of the helping process, for example, Egan; Carkhuff; Hamblin; Richard Nelson-Jones, the best known being Egan's three-stage model (see Further reading).

All helping approaches include skills that facilitate expression, awareness or understanding of feeling but, as becomes clear later, different approaches require different skills. The list of skills or guidelines below is based on Jacobs's classification (1999). Strictly speaking some guidelines are pointers towards what not to do rather than being a specific skill.

Guidelines for listening

Listening may suggest a passive act but it is actually an active process. It means listening with all the perceptual capacities. The listener needs to put aside any preoccupations and concerns about making a phone call; having to rush off to go to a meeting; or catching someone before they leave. If the teacher is preoccupied this may show by her looking at her watch, fiddling with her keys or sitting on the edge of her seat. If she feels under pressure to attend to someone the net result may be that the other person feels she is not really interested. It is far better for the teacher to say to a student that she has to teach in ten minutes or has to go to a meeting but she is willing to see them in her free period or at the end of the day, when she will have the time to listen carefully.

In general conversation, people often hear what they want to hear or find interesting, but that is not necessarily what is most important to the speaker. People tend to rehearse in their minds what they are going to say in response and thereby stop listening. In a counselling situation it is not a conversation that takes place. The pace is slower and there is more listening than responding, especially in the early stages. Rogers (1951: 349) sums this up well: 'Without attention there can be no understanding and hence no communication. Apparently the act of attending carefully to another person is a difficult task for most people. They are usually thinking what they will say when the speaker stops.' To be listened to, really listened to, is indeed quite rare. Many students say that more than anything they want the other person, be it a teacher, a parent or friend, just to listen and for them not to interrupt. So often the listener focuses on his reply or interrupts and the speaker is frustrated in her efforts to tell the other just how she feels.

There are several factors that impede listening. One relates to external noises and the other to internal distractions. With respect to external noises it may be difficult to concentrate when a class is waiting noisily in the corridor, a bell sounds, a phone rings or voices are carried through adjoining walls. With some forward planning some of these factors can be minimized, for example, by finding and using an appropriate room, stopping phone calls, putting notices on doors (see practical arrangements in Chapter 4).

The second form of distraction relates to internal preoccupations and this may be harder to tackle, since it requires a degree of self-awareness. Besides being aware of other demands, for example meetings or seeing colleagues, listening is impaired if the teacher is tired or ill, is only willing to follow certain lines of thought, judges the speaker or finds some subjects difficult to discuss. If the teacher finds certain topics embarrassing, painful or difficult her anxiety may be conveyed by her restlessness or by her quickly changing the subject. Such responses are picked up by the student, even though nothing is stated explicitly. Students will say, 'I could tell she wasn't really listening', or, 'I could tell she wasn't really wanting to hear what I was saying' (see self-awareness in Chapter 4).

A further barrier to good listening is the rate differential between speaking and thinking. People speak at about 150 to 250 words per minute, but they think three times faster. This means that most people tune in and tune out of conversations. Such selective tuning is inappropriate in counselling or the use of counselling skills because information may be filtered out according to personal bias. The aim is to listen to everything that is said. As Egan (1975: 69) says, 'good listening supplies him (the counsellor) with the building blocks of accurate empathy'.

Some writers suggest that counsellors need to learn to develop 'free floating attention' or the ability to listen to all that is being communicated. This means listening to the words, the metaphors, the volume, pitch, accent, tone of voice as well as observing facial expressions, bodily movements and eye contact. All such observations offer valuable clues about how the student feels. It is easier to pick up all this information if the teacher listens and thinks less about responding.

Moreover, if the teacher listens attentively she is more likely to pick up on themes that weave in and out of the discussion. These themes are very important, and tell the listener the student's major concerns. As Carkhuff and Pierce (1975: 39) state, 'The speaker will make the same points over and over in different ways. The themes tell us what the speaker is really trying to say about himself in relation to the world. They will tell us where he is "coming from" if we just provide him with the opportunity.'

Some micro-skills training models break down 'listening' into three component behaviours. They identify looking at the client and making eye contact; holding a relaxed posture; and responding in a way that conveys listening. Research does show that the combination of these three factors does indeed encourage expression of feelings and has a powerful reinforcing effect.

Remembering

It is easier to remember if the teacher listens rather than speaks. When she listens she can remember significant facts, specific words, and names. When she replies she can then convey her care and concern by mentioning important details. Most students feel valued when someone remembers their name and details about them. It is hard for a student to feel cared about if the teacher confuses her with someone else or does not remember significant details about her. It is far better for the teacher to say to a student that she has difficulty in remembering details and ask for a reminder than to try and bluff her way through a 'session' or an interview with a student.

Listening for underlying feelings

If feelings are straightforward people are usually able to manage them, even if they are distressing. For instance, grief is natural but it is more difficult to manage when mixed with guilt or relief. A student, Sarah, may say her dog has had to be put to sleep. 'He was old, but it's all for the best.' In this statement Sarah is rationalizing. She says it was for the best. Best for whom? Her parents? The dog? Her? It may be important to acknowledge that the dog was old, but nevertheless that he was a wonderful pet, he was greatly loved and will be missed. What may also be important is that Sarah may have other feelings that complicate the grieving process for her. She may feel guilty that she had neglected him recently because she had been busy with her friends. Feelings that could have been missed were that she was sad and feeling guilty.

In Paul's case he explains that his grandfather has just died, 'but he had a good innings'. Here feelings of loss are perhaps being denied. Feelings of sadness may be difficult for Paul to express and so he may try to avoid them. Perhaps Paul does not feel able to cry, or he may think it inappropriate for a boy to do so. His feelings may be further complicated by guilt – perhaps that he had not been to see his grandfather for a while. It is important to try to tune in to what is not being stated explicitly.

In Rachel's case she says her best friend has been picked for the county hockey trials and next season she, Rachel, may get picked too. Here Rachel may feel genuine pleasure for her friend but she may also feel great personal disappointment not to have been selected herself. It may be difficult to express this because she fears it will reflect poorly on herself as a friend. She may also feel envious, and such feelings may be uncomfortable and difficult to manage.

Sometimes an indication of underlying conflict is conveyed by a change in the tone of voice, by a sudden gesture or by a discrepancy between what is said and how it is said. For instance, Martin may say his friends are all going to the match on Saturday. Then he laughs and quickly adds that he does not mind not going because the team's going to lose anyway. He dismisses the event and denies how he really feels. Here it may be possible to pick up on Martin's feelings about not going, which may be about feeling rejected by his friends.

Listening involves more than just following the content of what is said. It involves listening to what is not being stated clearly, but is somehow being conveyed more subtly. If a teacher can respond to underlying feelings this conveys empathy. It is indeed a powerful experience to be listened to and to feel understood.

Attending to non-verbal communication

When students come to see a teacher a lot of important information can be picked up from the way they knock on the door, enter the room or sit on the chair, as well as from their clothes, general appearance, facial expressions, bodily movements, gestures and mannerisms. One student may knock loudly on the door, stride into the room and confidently sit down. Another taps gently on the door, hovers in the open doorway and sits hesitantly in the chair. Some students may take off their coat, huddle under it, pull it tightly around them or fold it carefully and lay it across their knees. Some students fidget and show their discomfort while others seem relaxed and at ease. All this information can be useful to understanding how a particular student feels. It is not surprising to learn that over half of all communication takes place non-verbally. In the classic study, Mehrabian (1971: 43) breaks down communication into:

- 7 per cent verbal, i.e. words only
- 38 per cent vocal, i.e. tone of voice, inflection
- 55 per cent non-verbal

Usually non-verbal behaviour supports what is being said. So that when Anne-Marie speaks quickly and says, 'I've got three projects to do and I need to arrange my work experience and I have to go and see the careers' teacher and . . .', she also makes expansive gestures and becomes breathless. The teacher then gets the impression that Anne-Marie is beginning to panic and feels rather overwhelmed. Or Anthony speaks slowly without much expression in his voice. He says, 'I'm so behind in my work. I've given up trying to do anything about it. I don't see the point in going to lessons because it just makes me feel worse. There's just no point in bothering.' As he does so he looks down at the floor and avoids giving eye contact. He conveys a consistent picture of someone who is disheartened and who may be depressed.

Of considerable value is spotting where what is being said in words is at odds with what is being conveyed non-verbally.

As a rule people can choose what they say but have very little control over what they communicate non-verbally. This discrepancy often highlights difficult feelings that the speaker may wish to hide, or avoid expressing. For instance, Sandip may say, 'Yes, I'm feeling relaxed about my exams. Everything is under control. No problems. Everything is fine. No sweat. I'm on schedule.' But as he speaks he tosses his head from side to side, avoids eye contact, and nods his head frequently. In such instances it can be helpful to pick up the discrepancy, and tactfully and gently say, 'I hear that you are telling me everything is going fine with your exams, but I'm wondering if I detect, deep down, that you may be rather worried.' Sandip may deny this, but he has been given an opportunity to explore how he really feels. He cannot be made to disclose how he feels and the hunch may be wrong. He may not be ready to talk about his feelings, but by making the suggestion tentatively, the teacher has not presumed to 'know', and the student may then decide to come back at a later time and share his anxieties.

Non-verbal communication can be broken down into several components, namely, body posture and gestures, facial expression and eye contact, and tone of voice. It needs to be remembered that there are differences as well as similarities between cultures and these are important to note and bear in mind. Each culture places its own norms and meanings on body posture, eye contact and distance. For example, in Middle Eastern culture eye-to-eye contact is permitted between two men but not between a man and a woman. Moreover sustained eye contact is considered offensive to some Native American groups. Unfortunately, much of the counselling literature refers to white British or American culture and insufficient attention has been paid to counselling in multiracial settings.

Body posture

Much useful information can be obtained by observing how a student sits, walks, or occupies her chair. For instance, Trish hovers in the doorway and waits to be told to sit down. She sits on the edge of the seat and twiddles with the zip on her coat. It can be helpful at such times to pick up on her nervousness and suggest, 'Perhaps you are rather worried about coming to see me today? I wonder if it will help you if I explain that we've got half an hour together and that you can just start talking about what's bothering you. To start with I'll just try and listen.'

It is normally possible to pick up sudden shifts in body posture. So that if a student suddenly folds her arms, sits back in the chair or crosses and uncrosses her legs such changes may indicate a change in feeling. For instance, if Trish sighs and sits back in her chair this indicates that she is already feeling more relaxed. If, however, she starts to talk about her concerns and then fidgets and looks away or crosses and uncrosses her legs she may be experiencing difficult feelings that again need recognizing. 'Trish, you seem to be quite anxious when you talk about how things are at home. I'm wondering if there is something really bothering you?'

Gestures and facial expression

Gestures can be said to be both genetically and culturally determined, but with many communication gestures the same all over the world. When someone is happy they smile and when they are angry they frown, or if someone shrugs their shoulders this universally implies that either a person does not know or does not understand. It is interesting that people are not taught gestures but learn them as part of the socialization process. According to Ekman *et al.* (1972) there are 76 gestures which are generally used and understood. Despite similarities between cultures there are also significant differences and this needs to be taken into account when working with groups or individual students of different origins.

One gesture may seem formal to one student but quite appropriate for another (for example, the handshake). Codes of behaviour vary, so that while Trish waits to be told to sit down, Sophie may automatically sit down. Some students use a lot of hand movements; they may wave their arms as they speak quite naturally, while another student may sit with her hands firmly clenched in her lap. Often there is no need to draw attention to the gesture itself, but to note what it seems to signify. The teacher may observe that when Martin is talking his body tenses up and he clenches his fists. The teacher may comment, 'I notice that when you speak about your stepfather you seem rather angry. Is this how you feel?'

A century ago the work of Darwin (1872) laid the foundation for theory and research on the facial patterns in emotion. Since then, facial patterns have been studied and found to be much the same in all cultures. The major difference between cultures lies in 'display' rules, or what is considered appropriate or inappropriate to show. For instance, the Japanese are not supposed to display anger or sadness; British boys and young men are discouraged from crying and showing their feelings.

In school, many children learn to straddle two cultures, but it is important for the dominant culture to make efforts to learn and understand about cultural differences and similarities. For example, Muslim girls may, as a sign of respect, be reluctant to make eye contact and from a British perspective this may be perceived as rude. Similarly the degree of physical proximity varies between cultures. Some prefer a greater or lesser distance between people. For middle-class white people in Britain, Australia, New Zealand and North America and Canada distance is usually similar, depending on whether the relationship is an intimate one, social or public. By contrast people from Latin American countries prefer far more closeness than many British people find acceptable.

The smile is said to be the most memorable facial expression, since it can express interest, benevolence and sympathy, although too much smiling can also indicate insincerity. Frequent frowning can be taken as showing disapproval whereas an occasional frown can indicate that a person is trying to understand or is puzzled. Further examples of facial expressions include twisted lips, smiles, frowns, blushes, temporary rashes or paleness. People are generally unaware of their facial expressions. It is important to remember that it is not only the students' behaviours that are being observed, but the student will also be observing the teacher!

The eyes reveal much about the way a person feels. According to Argyle (1983: 82) people typically engage in eye contact for about one-third of the time they are talking and 'look nearly twice as much while listening as while talking'. In counselling it is important to give intermittent eye contact to show the student that the teacher is listening and yet to look away from time to time to alleviate the intensity of the attention.

With regard to visually impaired students it is important to recognize that the main cues for turn taking in a conversation are mainly vocal, rather than visual, in much the same way as in a telephone conversation. There is a dearth of literature on the subject of counselling visually impaired people, but one of the research findings is that facial expressions are innate processes that need practice. Facial expressions in visually impaired people tend to be less well developed. Less information may be obtained from observing the face of a visually impaired speaker, and greater attention may need to be paid to tone of voice and loudness. Although the face is an important source of information it does not provide unique information. What is important to remember is that information that is not verbalized may be conveyed non-verbally in a variety of ways.

Information about how people feel is also conveyed through rapidity of speech, frequency of sighing and tone of voice. For instance, a depressed person speaks slowly and at a low and falling pitch. Someone who is anxious speaks quickly and unevenly in a raised pitch or maybe in a breathy voice, making a lot of speech errors. The voice may be loud and discordant or soft or easy to listen to. Loudness or softness when speaking on certain topics may be important clues to the strength of the feeling. A fast speech rate is generally associated with nervousness, while a slow rate may indicate depression. Sudden voice changes around certain topics can also be significant. In this sense, the voice, as Argyle (1983) suggests, is 'leakier' than the face, since strong emotions tend to show through.

There is no simple programme for learning how to read and interpret non-verbal communications. A working knowledge of non-verbal communication and its possible meanings is required, but it has to be remembered that there may be a number of interpretations. The key to understanding is the context. To be effective a helper needs to listen to the whole communication, and must test perceptions.

Listening to oneself

Sometimes this is called listening with the third ear (Reik 1948). It refers to the ability to use oneself although it does not mean disclosing details about oneself (see self-disclosure in Chapter 4). It involves trying to imagine how the other feels, and hence is the first step towards empathy. When Dean says, 'I haven't done my homework yet and I'm wondering if I can have an extension for my project?' it is important for the teacher to decide what stance she is going to take. She may feel critical, she may wonder why he is so disorganized, or she may feel he has had sufficient time. She may just want his work handed in. If she feels the matter bears further explanation it is important to put aside criticisms. It may be that Dean has got good reasons, and wants help. The teacher may say to Dean, 'Can you tell me a bit more about all this so that I can get a better picture of the problem. Then we can see if there's a helpful way forward?'

This shows that she is prepared to listen to his reasons. Some of the 'reasons' may not be very good, but if the teacher is trying to help him rather than lecture him on his disorganization, this may be an opportunity to improve his study skills. Criticizing him may temporarily satisfy the teacher but this does not actually help Dean. It may discourage him from approaching another teacher in the future.

On closer enquiry the teacher may find that Dean is under a lot of pressure at home. There may have been a new baby so that Dean has been required to take on more domestic responsibilities. There may be nowhere quiet to work at home, no desk, or simply a lack of encouragement in the family. It is important to think how the situation feels for Dean. If the teacher learns that Dean's father has just left home, the teacher needs to imagine how she would feel in such a situation. She might feel angry and sad that her father had left, angry with her mother for relying on her for practical and emotional support, and sad and angry that no one seems to recognize her distress. This 'imagining' or 'feeling into' is the first step towards making an empathic response (see empathic understanding in Chapter 3).

Allowing pauses and silences

Silence can mean many things and various studies have highlighted its complexity (Harper *et al.* 1978). Researchers show that silence is not the absence of response but the presence of extremely complex patterns of human interaction. Brammer and Shostrom (1968) point out that silence has beneficial values. They find that it can help a person talk; it allows a client to think and gain insights; and it slows down the pace of a session.

An interesting study quoted by Jacobs (1999) reveals that teachers tend to allow only 0.7 seconds for their students to answer questions addressed to them. The result is that only the quickest students answer; other children know the answer but need a little time to frame it, and so get passed over in favour of the quick ones. By training teachers to wait a few extra seconds the level of class participation was shown to rise.

In ordinary conversations there is a tendency to interrupt, but when using counselling skills there is a need to encourage more pauses and silences than usual. These allow both the speaker and the listener to take stock and reflect. For instance, Jane may come to see the teacher but then stay silent. The temptation is to set an agenda, or to ask her questions, but it is better to wait and then, if necessary, acknowledge her hesitation by saying, 'Perhaps you're wondering where to start. I'm happy for you to begin whenever you want to.' In this way a teacher is more likely to elicit Jane's concerns and her priorities.

With some children long silences can be experienced as uncomfortable. In counselling the use of silence is a specific skill, used advisedly. When using counselling skills it is important to allow brief silences and pauses, but not allow silence to become uncomfortable. After waiting a minute, the teacher may say to Jane, 'Perhaps you find it difficult to know where to start', or, 'You may find it hard to talk about your parents' separation.' Alternatively the subject may be distressing, and Jane fears she may get upset. The teacher could say, 'I imagine it is very upsetting for you at home at the moment. Perhaps you feel you are being disloyal to your parents by talking about how you feel.' The aim is to try to show understanding and convey empathy so that Jane feels encouraged to explore her feelings more fully.

In any situation it is important to assess what a silence means to the student. Sometimes it means the student is thinking about what has just been discussed, but it may also express fear, anger, boredom, respect, embarrassment or sadness. In order to assess the significance of the silence it is helpful to look at the non-verbal communication that accompanies it. Sometimes just commenting that a student seems tense, worried, angry or sad encourages a student to say more. Sometimes it is necessary to mention confidentiality to enable a student to feel safe enough to continue speaking. Simply acknowledging reticence to speak may also be helpful. 'I'm wondering if you are finding it difficult to say more about how you are feeling because you are not sure if you can trust me?', or, 'I'm wondering if you are reluctant to say anything because you feel angry that you've been sent to see me. Is that how it feels?'

Sometimes silences result from a misunderstanding, and this may need to be clarified. If the listener is 'in tune' with the speaker she will be able to 'feel' the silence and determine what the silence is in response to. A teacher herself needs to feel comfortable with pauses and silences, since by staying quiet she is in effect saying, 'I am listening. I am not afraid of the silence and I am going to give you space to reflect.' But if she rushes in to fill the space she effectively says, 'I don't like silences. They make me feel uncomfortable. I am not really focusing on your feelings.'

Silences can be interpreted as disapproving. This is more likely to happen when a student makes a personal disclosure and is anxious about the teacher's response. If Tim discloses that he is confused about his sexual identity he may be apprehensive about saying more, perhaps fearing a homophobic response. A silence could be experienced as discouraging or rejecting. A better response is to offer gentle encouragement. The teacher may say, 'Perhaps it is difficult for you to talk to me about your sexual feelings. I wonder if you are not really sure that I can understand how you feel?' In this situation it is important that a teacher feels comfortable about her own sexuality, and is not judgmental. If the teacher feels anxious, is unclear about such issues, or feels she is out of her depth, it is better to offer Tim the opportunity to speak to someone else, perhaps by saying, 'I'm not sure I'm the best person to talk to about this; I wonder what you would think about seeing the school counsellor or school nurse?', or, 'I've just been thinking about what you've been saying and I'm not sure I've got enough knowledge or experience in this matter, but I'm happy just to listen and then perhaps we can think whether or not it would be helpful to speak to someone who knows more about this? How does that sound to you?'

Occasions like this need to be handled sensitively since it is important that Tim does not feel rejected (see making a referral in Chapter 5). In this instance the issue may be more complicated by the fact that there may not be anyone in school to refer to and the task may be deciding together who would be the best agency, for example, the general practitioner (GP), Family Planning Clinic or a helpline. An unhelpful response to Tim is, 'I'm sure it's just a passing phase; you'll soon grow out of it.' This does not help Tim and it only serves to highlight the teacher's discomfort and lack of empathy and understanding. Indeed it may be that Tim is confused about his sexual feelings and may not be homosexual but a response that shows understanding for his confusion is better than a dismissal of his feelings.

Studies have shown that trainee counsellors and those learning counselling skills tend to speak before a client has stopped speaking, whereas experienced counsellors wait several seconds before responding. It may be that trainees are more anxious about their performance, or about making a good response, and that their anxiety interferes with the pacing of their responses. Allowing brief silences right from the first session sets the scene and the pace for subsequent sessions. If the teacher 'rescues' the student from a short silence in the first session, a precedent will have been created that may be difficult to change.

There is a danger that in responding too quickly the listener changes the direction of the discussion, or worse still changes the subject. In certain situations, if the speaker suddenly falls silent or stops and glances to one side, it can be helpful to ask, 'What are you feeling now?' This conveys an awareness that there has been a discernible shift of thought or feeling that might indicate that the speaker has realized something important, or recalled a memory that she is considering whether to share.

Relaxing and staying calm

A teacher's demeanour and the physical surroundings should convey calm. It is important to pay attention to the room, seating, privacy, freedom from interruptions. The essential ingredient is showing calm even if the speaker is talking about upsetting matters. The aim is to contain the feelings, and to demonstrate that feelings are manageable. For instance, Tina says she is pregnant. She says she feels awful, panicky, scared and confused. Initially the teacher's task is to listen and explore what Tina is feeling before going on to look at what she is going to do. The teacher may feel upset and concerned, but her priority is to contain her own feelings and help Tina look at hers and then decide on a course of action. Such a calm and accepting response greatly helps. Tina may fear her teacher's disapproval, or she may fear what will happen to her. She may feel desperate. Her teacher's relaxed concern will help her.

The teacher may say, 'Okay Tina, let's look at this together. Perhaps you can tell me a bit more about the situation.' She may decide to enquire further about her boyfriend and her parents and so say, 'Before we can decide on a course of action I think it will help me to know a bit more especially about your parents and your boyfriend.' After a while the teacher can continue, 'Now you've told me how you think your parents will react and what your boyfriend says, but I'm interested to hear about how you feel about being pregnant?' The teacher may go on to explore Tina's options, 'I'm wondering about ideas you've had so far about being pregnant.' It is vital that Tina arrives at her own decision. If she senses the teacher thinks one option is preferable to another this may colour Tina's responses and complicate the decision-making process. At such times it is most important for the teacher to monitor her own responses. By structuring the exploration with Tina it becomes possible for her to examine her own feelings in safety.

More disturbing would be the revelation that Sandra has been raped. This situation requires extreme tact and is likely to make the teacher feel more anxious because of her own horror and because of the element of urgency about the problem. Here again it is very important for the teacher to stay calm and demonstrate her willingness to listen. She needs to contain her own feelings, particularly paying attention to her own facial expressions, body posture, body movements and gestures, all of which may convey her discomfort and alarm.

Staying calm on the surface is also helpful when dealing with angry students or angry parents. The anger can be acknowledged by saying, 'I can see you are very angry but if I could just listen while you try to explain to me what has led up to this, then perhaps I can understand and even help.' By recognizing the feeling straight away and showing a willingness to hear the other's point of view a teacher can begin to diffuse the situation and look at the problem constructively. Meeting anger with anger, or irritability with irritability, often escalates the situation.

For example, Mr Green complains noisily at a parents' evening that the form tutor has not been keeping a check on Trevor's attendance and behaviour and that his grades are low, and he looks like failing all his exams. The teacher may feel tempted to explain just how much effort has been put in on Trevor's account. The important point is to pick up on Mr Green's concerns and his feelings, and then look at the problem in a constructive way. The teacher may say, 'I can tell you are angry about the situation. Perhaps you feel disappointed in the way I have handled this matter, but I'm wondering if we can look at each problem in turn and see what has or hasn't happened, and what might be the best way forward.' It may make the teacher uncomfortable to deal with an irate parent at a public event, but her objective is to stay calm even though she may feel angry, upset or anxious.

Summary

Some people may regard listening as passive behaviour but it is actually an active process. It takes concentration and discipline to listen property. Listening can be taught as a set of techniques or micro-skills which at first may seem artificial, but in time become natural responses. Practice and feedback are necessary to develop these skills. I have shown in many of my examples how good listening and observation can lead to more appropriate responses. Ways of responding are equally necessary skills to learn in helping students. It is these which I develop further in the next chapter.

Chapter 3

Responding skills

Guidelines for responding

Reflecting feelings

Putting feelings into words can be difficult for many people because they do not have an extensive vocabulary for expressing feelings. Some people say they are 'depressed' which might mean they are suffering from a clinical depression, or that they are feeling low or fed up at that particular time. Similarly angry feelings can range from rage and hate to annoyance and irritation. In a helping context it is important to try to find or define the right degree of a feeling or emotion. This is done by clarifying what a particular word might mean and by reflecting what has been understood by that word. For example, if Lee says he is 'depressed' it is important to find out how long he has been feeling like that and in relation to what. If he says he has felt like this for months since breaking up with Emma, the picture is quite different from saying he feels like this today, because he has been given a detention.

It is very important to show that what has been said has been heard and understood. So when Jane tells you her parents are getting a divorce the teacher can show her understanding by responding with, 'That must be terribly upsetting for you', or, 'That must be very worrying and upsetting for you.' When Lee says he is depressed because he and Emma have split up you can say, 'I can see you are very upset about it. Would it be helpful to tell me more about it?' It is not helpful to say, 'Oh well, never mind. I'm sure you will get over it soon.' Reassurance that things will be all right are usually said for the benefit of the helper and effectively close down further discussion. The implied message is that this area is either too difficult or unimportant to be discussed.

If the 'wrong' word is selected by a teacher the student may deny a particular feeling. For instance, if Anne-Marie says her friends went to a party without her, the teacher may say, 'I guess you felt angry about that.' Where the rapport is good Anne-Marie may then explain, 'Well, I'm not so much angry as hurt that they didn't tell me.' At such times it is important that the teacher does not attribute a feeling to a student that she herself might have. Being empathic means trying to understand a situation as if the listener was the other person, not imagining how the listener would feel in that situation.

The purpose of reflecting a feeling is to focus on the feeling rather than on the content alone (paraphrasing). It is particularly helpful to bring vaguely expressed feelings into clearer awareness. This helps both the teacher and the student. For example, 'You say you're fed up and want to leave home, that you've had enough of your stepfather. But I detect some hesitation in your voice, is that right?' The student then knows that the teacher has listened and has understood. But, if there is a misunderstanding, this can be cleared up quickly.

It can be very helpful to reflect observations about a student's non-verbal behaviour and say, 'Jane, you say you feel it is all for the best that your Mum and Dad are going to get a divorce, because they are rowing all the time and home is so unpleasant now, but I notice you sigh a lot and look wistful as you speak. Perhaps you also feel sad about their decision?' The last part is put tentatively. It allows space for Jane to agree or disagree and for the subject to be explored further. To Anne-Marie the teacher may say, 'I see you are smiling when you tell me your friends go out together and don't invite you; I wonder if I also sense that inside you are really hurting.' How well the teacher reflects feelings largely depends on her ability to be sensitive.

Sometimes a teacher can block exploration by inappropriate responses. When Aisha says she feels really fed up to be back at school after the holidays, it is not helpful to say, 'Yes, I know what you mean. I always feel like that after Christmas. Perhaps it is the time of year.' Or, 'We all feel like that sometimes, especially after a holiday.' By making either of those responses Aisha is denied the opportunity of saying what it is like for her. Similarly if Tim says he's not looking forward to the summer holidays, an unhelpful reply is to say, 'Oh I am. I'll be going away and will have time to read a couple of novels.' This does not help Tim and may even make him feel worse. It is more helpful to reply, 'Can you tell me more about what the summer holidays mean for you, Tim?'

By reflecting feelings the aim is to try to understand what a student is saying and to encourage her to say more. Rogers (1951: 113) describes this process of trying to be with the client graphically: 'the therapist becomes a companion to the client as the latter searches through a tangled forest in the dead of night. The therapist responses are more in the nature of calls through the darkness; Am I with you? Is this where you are? Are we together?' It is difficult and perhaps inappropriate to adopt this style in normal conversation but the use of counselling skills is very different from a normal conversation. There is much more freedom and space for the client to speak, and less need for the helper to speak about her experiences.

The analogy of an emotional mirror is often used in the counselling literature and is a useful one. If the helper can reflect feelings as they are expressed without distortion, a student can begin to make sense of her feelings. For instance, a teacher can say, 'It sounds as if you really hate your stepfather', or, 'It looks as though you are really angry.' It is unhelpful to say, 'Oh I'm sure you don't really hate him.' Such statements imply that it is wrong to hate and effectively stifle further discussion. It is far better to acknowledge a feeling, discuss how it has arisen and then help the student make sense of it. If the teacher can accept the strength of different feelings, this can help the student learn they are normal and manageable.

Sometimes it is important to acknowledge that a student has contradictory feelings, such as both love and hate. By normalizing such mixed feelings a student is spared from feeling guilty and confused. For instance the teacher can say, 'You seem to have two feelings about your mother. You love her but you also hate the way she restricts your independence.' Allowing students to own and express these feelings helps them to develop tolerance and understanding about the complexity of their responses to significant people in their lives.

Reflecting feelings is sometimes considered one of the hardest skills to master. There may be cultural and gender differences in that some people do not readily or easily talk about certain feelings. This needs to be understood and respected. In the role of helper it is important to feel comfortable about them in order to help others explore their feelings safely. The real skill is to find a personal style and a personal language. Not every sentence needs to be reflected back. Sometimes a nod or 'Mm' will suffice. Responses need to vary so that they remain genuine. It has been found that a common error in learning to reflect feelings is to deliver responses in a repetitive way, for example, 'You feel, you seem, it seems to be.' Language needs to be appropriate to the age, ability and experience of the student. The tone should be natural and simple, neither patronizing nor involving complex sentences or technical jargon. Allowances are made by students for slightly inaccurate responses so long as the student senses a genuine desire to help and understand.

Empathic understanding

This skill is central to all counselling skills. Without empathy a student does not feel encouraged to reveal more about how she feels. Making an empathic response is an active appreciation of a student's feeling or experience. Empathy needs to be conveyed sensitively and tentatively because the teacher cannot be sure what the student feels. Phrases such as 'perhaps' or 'I'm not sure but . . .' can be helpful. For instance, when Gulshan says she is moving house the teacher may pick up two feelings about the event. She may say, 'You seem very accepting about moving house, but I wonder if you might also be feeling sad?' Gulshan may then feel able to say that there are many advantages to moving for the family, but from her point of view she will be leaving the house she was born in and has lived in all her life. It may be difficult to talk about those feelings to her parents because they are so pleased about the move and she suspects they may think her silly and immature for not wanting to leave the house.

Whenever a teacher uses counselling skills it is important for her to monitor her own feelings. So that when Sally says her family are moving yet again, this time to another town so she'll have to start at a new school, the teacher may think this is sad for Sally since she has only just settled and another upheaval will be very difficult for her. The teacher may feel critical of the parents for moving her again. Moreover, this situation may also trigger memories in the teacher's own life about moving and changing schools; she may have feelings that moves are inevitable or avoidable, exciting or stressful, good or bad. What is important is that the teacher's response is not coloured by her personal feelings and personal experiences, but that the teacher tries to listen and understand how it is for Sally.

Divided loyalties are often present, as in Gulshan's case. What seems best for the family may not feel good for her. Similarly with Sally she may feel she has little power and influence and may accept it is her parent's decision. But she may be feeling very anxious, and reluctant to say anything to her parents for fear of upsetting them. An inappropriate response to Sally or Gulshan would be to say, 'Oh, how lovely. How exciting!' By the same token offering personal memories of house moving is not helpful, 'Oh I remember when we moved house. We lived out of boxes for months and never seemed to know where anything was.' These responses may show that the teacher has had a similar experience and is willing to share them, but this is not empathy. It is not feeling the way into how it is for Gulshan or Sally. The focus in such a response is on the teacher and her experience. Although there may be similarities, this does not allow the student to explore the problem from her perspective.

If the teacher really wants to bring herself into the conversation she could say, 'Oh yes I remember moving house. I had such mixed feelings about it, happy and sad. I wonder what you're feeling?', or, 'I was once in that situation and I found I had such mixed feelings.' Here the teacher returns the focus to the student, and the time the student has to listen to the teacher is kept to a minimum. The disadvantage of describing personal experience is that while the event may be similar, the feelings are not necessarily the same. This is particularly significant if the student is from a different cultural background. However hard a teacher tries to understand a situation, she may have to acknowledge that she simply does not know what it is like to be black, Asian, disabled, gay or male, and cannot know what their experience of the event is like. Accurate empathy is even more difficult to achieve if the experience being described is totally unfamiliar, making it important to listen carefully and not make assumptions or generalizations.

If the teacher feels unsure about what a student is saying about a particular situation, but has a sense of a particular feeling, for example of disappointment, she can say, 'Some people may feel disappointed about that, but I don't know if that's how it is for you?' In essence, trying to respond empathically means trying to show that the helper has been listening and has also been trying to understand how the other person feels.

Using questions

The focus of many non-counselling interviews, for example with a solicitor, doctor or careers adviser, largely consists of questions and answers to elicit as much factual information as possible in the time available. When using counselling skills, although it is important to gather some information, the emphasis is much more on allowing expression of feeling.

'Closed' questions can be used when an answer to a specific question is required. 'Open' questions can be used when exploration and discussion are encouraged. For example, 'Which subjects do you intend to take at A level?' is a closed question, which requires a precise answer, but, 'What are your thoughts about staying on at school after the summer?' is an open question because it invites discussion about GNVQs or A levels or even leaving school altogether.

If Miriam says she is 'fed up', to ask 'Why?' is to ask a closed question. The chances are that Miriam does not know, and responds, 'I dunno'. A teacher can ask a semi-open question and say, 'How long have you been feeling fed up?' But a more open question would be, 'Can you tell me more about feeling so fed up?' If Miriam says she has not been getting much sleep lately, and feels tired all the time, it is unhelpful to say, 'Is that because you've been going out a lot?', or, 'Is that because you've been going to bed late?' These responses suggest the teacher knows the answer and also implies the criticism or judgement that all teenagers go to bed late and do not want to get up in the morning. It may transpire that there's a new baby in the house; or she is being a perfectionist with her work; or she is depressed. It is important to remember that the teacher is not putting herself into the role of a doctor, but simply trying to see if this is an ongoing problem that may need a doctor's opinion or is a temporary phenomenon due to stress or a hectic social life.

If Miriam's sleeping has been a problem for some weeks or even months, it is helpful to enquire if her parents or her doctor are aware of this. The teacher can ask, 'Have you thought about mentioning this to your parents or your GP?' This is more tactful than saying, 'I think you ought to go and see your GP', or, 'You must tell your parents.' Much depends on the tone of voice, but encouragement is needed rather than firm advice. The danger of giving advice is that if the advice is not taken (and it may, of course, be the wrong advice) the student may not feel able to return to discuss the problem further (see giving information later in this chapter).

If the problem is to do with Miriam being over-meticulous it may be possible to explore her work patterns to determine the extent of the problem. Again asking 'why' she spends four hours on her homework is not helpful. Her answer may simply be that it takes that long. The teacher may need to ask some closed questions to elicit factual information, for example, 'How long do you spend each night on your homework?', 'What time do you work until at night?', or, 'Do you allow yourself any breaks or relaxation periods?' Nevertheless too many questions can be experienced as attacking.

As a rule 'why' questions are best avoided. Too easily they can put the student on the defensive, as if they indicate criticism and disapproval. The student feels she has to give a legitimate or acceptable reason, which may or may not be the real answer. If a teacher asks, 'Why are you late?' there may be little opportunity to tell the truth. Reasons abound such as, 'My Dad's alarm never went off', or, 'My Mum overslept', or, 'The bus was late.' Teachers have heard hundreds of excuses, some of them quite creative, but it is often difficult for a student to say what actually happened, for fear of receiving a lecture in return.

Where the teacher takes a step beyond asking 'why', and enquires further, the response may be different. Instead of saying, 'Why are you always late in the morning?' it may be more productive to say, 'I wonder what it is that stops you being here on time in the morning?' This recognizes the pattern of lateness and seeks to open up the discussion to see if there is a problem that can be explored.

Again, if Dean regularly does not give his work in on time, instead of asking 'why', it is more productive to say, 'It seems to me that there's a problem here. I'm wondering if I can help in any way? Do you think it would be useful for me to look at your work?' He may decline the offer on this occasion, but may come back later. He may go on to say that he was reluctant to ask for help; he had family worries; he felt stupid; he did not understand; or even that he cannot see the point of doing the work because he knows he is going to fail anyway. With this information the teacher is in a better position to tackle the problem.

Generally speaking, open questions are best used when an opinion, explanation or example is needed. The question is best kept short and direct so that it does not impede the flow of the discussion. Questions beginning with 'what' or 'how' are usually open as well as 'would' or 'could' which invite cooperation. Closed questions, on the other hand, close down discussion by demanding an answer. Questions beginning with 'is', 'are', 'do', 'did', 'who', 'when' are closed. Consider the difference between these two questions. 'Do you get on with your parents?' and 'How do you get on with your parents?' A helpful point to remember is that on the whole closed questions focus on the concerns of the questioner and in so doing the questioner may not really listen to the student. Open questions centre around the student's concerns and help her clarify her problems.

There is another way to put a question, which if done too often can sound artificial. If the last word or key words are reflected back as a question this can be very effective. It serves to encourage the student to carry on talking. For example, 'I hate it at home. My Mum nags me all the time to do jobs around the house.' The teacher can say, 'She nags you?' Or if David says, 'I hate the lunch breaks. It all gets me down. Only Wednesdays are okay', the teacher may say, 'Wednesdays are okay?' In a way, such questions serve as minimal prompts to facilitate further explorations. The tone of voice and the inflection in the voice are important and show the teacher is listening and wants the student to carry on and say more.

A final point to bear in mind is that too many questions can feel inquisitorial. The teacher may obtain a lot of factual data, but the student is unlikely to feel that her concerns have been understood. Moreover if, at the first meeting, the teacher asks a lot of questions largely arising out of her own nervousness, this pattern is easily established and may be difficult to change in subsequent meetings.

Minimal prompts

At first these interjections seem rather insignificant. In practice they serve to encourage the student to continue speaking. They show that the teacher is listening and does not want to interrupt. In effect they say, 'Yes, I'm listening', or, 'Carry on.' Other prompts include, 'Go on', 'Aha', 'Mm', 'Yes', 'So'.

Non-verbal signals such as a nod or a hand gesture also serve the same purpose. As stated above, reflecting a key word back in question form can also serve as a minimal prompt. For example, if Paul says, 'My grandfather went into hospital at the weekend', the teacher can say, 'Into hospital?'; or if Helen says, 'It was all going really well until last night', the teacher can say, 'Until last night?'

Paraphrasing

Repeating the last few words often prompts a student to carry on speaking, but at times paraphrasing is useful. This shows not only that the teacher is listening to what is being said, but also that she has understood correctly. There is a clear difference between paraphrasing and reflecting. A paraphrase captures the content of what has been said while a reflecting statement conveys the feeling; for example, if Samantha is clearly anxious and says she has to choose between seeing her Dad this weekend or going to a party with her friends, the teacher may respond, 'You seem to have difficulty in making a choice' (paraphrasing), or, 'You seem rather apprehensive about making a decision' (reflecting).

Paraphrasing is a way of restating accurately what has been said in similar but fewer words and it can also serve to summarize the content (see summarizing later in this chapter). Paraphrasing allows students to hear their thoughts reflected back to them and to hear how they sound. Sometimes a combination of paraphrasing and reflecting can be used very effectively; for example, 'Well, Mrs Fielding, let me see if I have understood you correctly. You say you feel this school has little to offer Stephen and that you are angry and disappointed in the lack of special provision for Stephen.' By its very starkness Mrs Fielding is obliged to look at what she has been saying. In this context the teacher is not putting her interpretation on what Mrs Fielding has been saying, but is both paraphrasing the content and reflecting back her feelings. This can be more effective than taking a defensive stance, such as listing all the good points of the school, and what time and effort has been put in to help Stephen. The aim of the latter is to justify the teacher's position, with the hope of changing Mrs Fielding's viewpoint. But it is unlikely that any arguments will be heard by Mrs Fielding until her feelings have been acknowledged. If a heated exchange ensues, the issues could easily be lost in the struggle to win the argument.

By recapping on what Mrs Fielding has said and by picking up her feelings of anger and disappointment, the teacher is showing that she is trying to appreciate the problem from Mrs Fielding's point of view. Then there is a possibility of exploring what the school has tried, what has or has not been effective, and what options are still available. Once Mrs Fielding's point of view has been heard and understood it may be possible to look at resources and funding, and move towards a constructive solution.

In another situation Tina says she is pregnant, but gives so much detail that the teacher feels confused. She decides to paraphrase to check out her understanding: 'Now let me see if I understand what you've been telling me. You think you are pregnant. You're not actually sure because although you used a condom, it split and you haven't actually taken a pregnancy test. Is that right?' Here the teacher seeks to clarify the facts of the problem rather than focus on the feelings. However, if Winston says he needs somewhere to live because of family problems the teacher may paraphrase the conversation and reflect the feelings: 'You seem to be saying that you've got mixed feelings about staying at home. You want to stay at home with your Mum and your younger brothers and sisters, but you and your stepfather just don't get on at all. Is that how it is?'

When Sandra says, 'I really love my mum, she does lots of things for me, she washes and irons my clothes, and gives me money. But she nags me a lot when I go out with my friends and treats me as if I'm still a kid', her teacher could respond, 'It sounds like you appreciate all that your Mum does for you (paraphrase) but I sense that you also feel she is a bit over-protective. Is that so?' (reflecting). If Sandra goes on to say, 'Well, one minute she's really nice to me and then half an hour later she yells at me for not tidying my room', the teacher can then paraphrase this: 'You think she's rather inconsistent?'

A paraphrase is quite different from an interpretation, which is a construction of the facts or feelings from the point of view of the listener. It is also different from a summary in which a significant portion of dialogue is condensed. As a consequence of hearing a paraphrase students know they are being understood and feel encouraged to carry on. If the paraphrase is not accurate any misunderstanding needs to be clarified. As with all responses it is important to find fresh ways of making similar statements, for example, 'Am I right in thinking . . ?' is one way of putting it, and, 'You seem to be saying . . ?' is another.

Avoid making judgements or loaded remarks

It is best to avoid expressing verbal or non-verbal exclamations of surprise, disgust or intolerance. As a good listener the aim is to show understanding through empathic responses. Some non-verbal indicators may 'leak' out, for example the raised eyebrow, the eyes widening. The teacher may be horrified, disgusted or shocked, but it is important for her not to reveal her real feelings unless she has thought out her reasons for doing this.

It may be that a student is 'testing' a teacher before deciding whether or not it is safe to continue talking. Jane says that at a party recently some of her friends drank too much alcohol and smoked cannabis. She knows this is illegal, and the question the teacher needs to ask herself is why Jane is telling her this now. If the teacher appears disapproving and critical she may be reluctant to say more. Instead, if the teacher is calm and gently makes further enquiries, Jane may reveal her actual worries. The teacher can respond, 'I wonder what you made of the party', or, 'It sounds as if you're not altogether happy about that. Perhaps you'd like to say more about it – you don't have to tell me the names of your friends.' Jane may then feel able to discuss her dilemma, without feeling she is betraying her friends. Because the incident was out of school the ethical dilemma for the teacher is different and somewhat more straightforward than had the incident taken place in school.

Eventually Jane may feel safe enough to state her dilemma. She may say she feels divided loyalties. She does not want to betray her friends but she is scared about getting involved with drugs. If the teacher responds immediately by saying, 'Well Jane, you know taking cannabis is illegal, you don't want to get involved in that stuff. It will ruin your life. Take my advice and stay away from drugs', then Jane may feel it is not possible to discuss her problem. The teacher needs to remember that students usually ask for help when they are experiencing some conflict. Jane knows what she 'ought' to do. She knows 'doing drugs' is illegal and she knows her parents would disapprove, but she needs time to explore the other side, her curiosity and her loyalty to her friends. Any comments such as 'Drugs are dangerous', or 'Soft drugs lead to harder drugs', disapproving gestures or facial expressions do not actually help Jane explore her dilemma. She may have decided to test the teacher more directly and said, 'What do you think about taking drugs, Miss?', but she will probably know that teachers disapprove of drugs. The skill is to look beyond the immediate question to the concerns behind it.

On a different issue, that of sexual promiscuity, the teacher may again be tempted to reveal her personal opinions, or convey her disapproval by her tone of voice or facial expressions. Hayley may say she's had loads of boyfriends and that sex is good fun – part of a good night out, like going to the pub. She says it is stupid treating sex as something special, just for marriage. She does not know what all the fuss is about. The teacher may be tempted to talk about health risks, or the disadvantages of earning such a reputation, or the inadvisability of treating relationships so casually. But again she needs to ask herself why Hayley is saying this and saying it so defiantly. Any effort to point out the dangers involved in promiscuous behaviour only sounds like moralizing. Instead the focus needs to be on what Hayley feels about her behaviour. Some health education may come into the discussion later, but initially a calm response to what she is saying is needed.

If the teacher concentrates on what Hayley says and does not respond to it, but instead listens to what underlying communication there is, then there is scope for exploration. For instance, the teacher may say, 'I'm just wondering, Hayley, if you are saying that sex is good but ordinary; and you are confused that some people see it as special.' Hayley may want to create an impression of sexual permissiveness; she may want to shock people (including the teacher), but she may also feel very insecure about relationships. She may feel trapped in a pattern of behaviour or be scared about contacting HIV or Aids. It is unhelpful to begin, 'You know you could catch Aids or HIV from sleeping around', or to show disapproval in other ways. It is better to respond, 'I'm wondering if there is something about what you've just told me that is bothering you but you're worried that I'll give you a lecture about contraception or health education?'

Similarly if Tim says he is gay and is thinking about telling his peer group, it is important not to respond with surprise or shock but to listen to his concerns and help him explore them. The teacher may be concerned about a student 'coming out', for a variety of reasons including, for example, a prevailing homophobic climate in the school, or because the student has not yet thought through the ramifications of such a disclosure. It is certainly not helpful to say, 'Oh I wouldn't do that Tim!', or, 'You'd be making a big mistake if you did that.' A more helpful response is, 'Okay, Tim. I understand that you feel ready to "come out". I wonder if it might be helpful to look at the possible reactions in your friends first.'

A different dilemma may arise if Tina says she is pregnant and is thinking about having an abortion. She may not know whether a teacher is (for example) a Catholic who is against abortion. It may be very difficult for such a teacher to help Tina with this decision but if this is the case it is unhelpful to say, 'I am totally against abortions under any circumstances.' It is more helpful for a teacher to state where she stands on this issue if she is going to be personally compromised, and so reply, 'I'm not sure I am the best person to help you with this dilemma, because I am a Catholic and I don't want you to feel influenced by my beliefs. I wonder if it would be more helpful to speak to someone else about this? I will be interested to hear what you decide to do, but I am not sure if I can be objective.'

As a rule it is best to avoid making judgements or expressing personal opinions since they effectively close down discussion. For instance, Paul says he is not sure about going to his grandfather's funeral on Friday. The teacher may have strong feelings about this and respond too quickly with, 'Oh you must go, Paul. You might regret it if you don't', or, 'Oh you must go. I always regretted not going to my grandfather's funeral.' Both responses tell Paul what he should do, but they do not help him explore his uncertainties. A better response is, 'I wonder if it would be helpful to look at the advantages and disadvantages of going and not going; and see what comes up before making a decision', or, 'I wonder if you can tell me what thoughts you have had about going or not going?'

Any teacher has her or his own thoughts and feelings about attending funerals, sexual relationships, drugs, abortion, alcohol and so on, but in a helping capacity the teacher does not impose values and beliefs on to the student. The aim instead is to help the student explore her own behaviour values and conflicts, and help her find her own solutions, even where this may not be in accordance with a teacher's beliefs and values.

Sharing personal information is inadvisable for several reasons. First, it takes the focus away from the student. Second, although the event or issue (abortions, pregnancy, use of drugs or alcohol) may be one the teacher has experienced, the feelings may be quite different. Third, it is a breach of personal boundaries, preventing the relationship from being professional. Fourth, such information may prove too much of a burden for the student to hold, like a 'secret', and although it was intended for that student only, it may be passed on inappropriately to other students. Empathy and understanding can be conveyed accurately without making personal revelations (see self-disclosure in Chapter 4).

When listening to a student it is also important not to show impatience. A student may be repeating herself or going round in circles and the teacher may feel like saying, 'Oh come on Miriam, we've been going over this time and time again, I think it's time you made your mind up one way or another. I haven't got time to spend going round and round.' A more effective response is, 'We seem to be going round in circles. I wonder if we can stop and look at why that is happening?' Even if the teacher feels impatient, had it been easy to arrive at a decision Miriam would have done so already. Decisions are complicated by such thoughts as, 'What will others think of me?', 'What will happen if I make the wrong choice?', or, 'How can I do what I want in this situation?' Sometimes the inability to make decisions indicates underlying depression.

Linking experiences

By employing all the different skills described so far, most students can be helped to look at their problems and to find their own solutions. The understanding can be taken a step further by connecting present experiences with similar experiences in the past. Such linking is a simple form of making an interpretation, as is used in more formal counselling.

It becomes clear with some people that certain problems are being repeated over and over again, and it can be extremely effective to make this clear. Such observations need to be offered tactfully and gently. For instance, Miriam says she has fallen out with her friends, and that they are giving her dirty looks in the corridors. She goes on to say that she is not bothered, because she will soon make new friends. She always does. After gentle encouragement she says this has happened before. It happened at her old school, and before that at her primary school. She just moves on to a different group of friends. Tactfully the teacher can suggest, 'You say this has happened before and is happening again now. I wonder if you've got any ideas about why this happens.' It can be fairly straightforward to identify the connection between what is happening now and what has happened in the past. The difficult part is making the connection sensitively, so that it can be heard and thought about rather than rejected outright.

Sometimes a teacher may remind the student of someone significant in the student's past or current life, for example, a parent or a step-parent. Paula may say, 'I can't bear Mrs Singer.

She doesn't like me and is always picking on me and never wants to help me.' At such times it can be helpful to say, 'Let's look at this, Paula, and see what goes on between you and Mrs Singer.' It is possible that Mrs Singer does not like Paula, but it may also be that Mrs Singer reminds Paula of her stepmother. The intensity of Paula's feelings may provide a clue to the fact that the problem is not just to do with Mrs Singer. If this is the case, further discussion can follow.

Sometimes links can be made when a student experiences a loss, such as the death of a pet, or moving house or changing school. If Sarah seems profoundly distressed after the death of her dog it may be because her grief has tapped into her loss of her grandmother a year earlier. It may also transpire that at the time of her grandmother's death Sarah felt she had to be very grown-up and brave, because her mother was so distressed herself. Making links between events now and events in the past is a way of making sense of intense feelings and experiences.

These links involve presenting the student with a new frame of reference, through which the student can view her problems, and hopefully better understand and deal with them. An interpretation comes from a listener's frame of reference and so is different from paraphrasing or reflecting. It is not necessarily the true meaning of events, but it is a construction of them and an understanding from the listener's perspective. The timing of such interpretations is vital, since even if the link and construction is correct, it can be rejected if it is badly timed. Interpretations are based on information gleaned over a period of time, and are not wild guesses.

Avoiding changing the subject

Changes and shifts in subject are possible clues that several things are going on for a student. To begin with, the teacher can allow the student to move from one subject to another, but after a while it may be necessary to encourage her to focus on one problem at a time. Equivocation indicates the student's discomfort and anxiety, but by listening attentively she can be helped to relax and become more focused. The teacher can say, 'I understand that you have got several things bothering you: your relationship with your boyfriend, your relationships at home, and the fact that you're moving house. I'm wondering if it would be helpful to look at each one in turn?'

The disadvantage of letting a student ramble about a whole series of issues is that the conversation will feel chaotic both to the student and the teacher, who may often feel swamped by the number of concerns. Often simple recognition that there are several worrying issues is calming. The suggestion of a review, each problem in turn, can introduce a sense of control and management. For instance, if Paula presents a whole series of issues, it might be helpful to say, 'I can see that you've got a lot of things on your mind. I'm not sure we'll have time to look at each of them today but I wonder if we can start by looking at the one that seems to worry you most?' It is important for Paula to decide which is most worrying for her. On the teacher's scale of things what she concentrates upon may not seem like the most important issue (for example, homework or project work), but it is essential that Paula takes some control and presents what she perceives as her most worrying problem.

Similarly the teacher will need to notice her own anxiety, to be aware if she is changing the subject because a topic is too upsetting for her. A student will detect if the teacher finds a subject too painful to discuss, and is therefore unable to explore that matter further. If a subject is raised which the teacher finds difficult, the teacher needs to work on her reactions including any feelings that are being stirred up. There are times when consultation or supervision of counselling work is necessary (see support in Chapter 4).

If the subject being discussed is painful or difficult, and the teacher notices the student sidetracking with a lot of irrelevant detail, it can be useful to remark, 'I think we are wandering away from what we have been talking about. I realize it is a painful topic but you were saying that . . .'. Stay with one major theme or problem at a time and avoid sudden shifts or change of subject, but also recognize the reason for changing topic may be because it is too hard to stay with.

Avoiding speaking too often, for too long

When responding to a student it is best to keep replies simple and brief. Lengthy responses prevent the teacher from listening and attending to the student, and are difficult to follow, especially when the student is upset, anxious or confused. It can feel more like a tutorial than a counselling session. Interruptions should be kept to a minimum.

Summarizing

Summarizing entails crystallizing what has been said. It differs from reflecting feelings and paraphrasing although it may include both elements. Summarizing gives structure to what has been expressed, and is often used to emphasize important points or to conclude a session and highlight the key areas discussed. Since a summary may not be altogether accurate it is important to listen for some confirmation, so that if there is any misunderstanding it can be sorted out there and then. Phrases such as, 'Is this so?' or, 'Am I right?', or, 'Have I understood you so far?' provide this opening.

The timing of a summary is important. It might interrupt the flow of dialogue, but it can be helpful after a student has spoken at length, or made a confusing or contradictory remark. Just before the end of the meeting it can be particularly helpful in recapping and clarifying any agreements. For instance, 'Well Lisa, we've got about five minutes left and I'd like to make sure we're both clear about what we've agreed to do. I will speak to your personal tutor about your coursework between now and Thursday and you will speak to your parents about changing your options and then on Friday we'll meet together again and review the situation. Is that how you've understood our discussion?' 'Let me sum up how I've understood things and you tell me if I've got anything wrong, is that okay?' 'Let's see. You are going to speak to your Mum about the dates of your holidays and then you're going to contact the day nursery to see when you could work there and then you'll contact me. You think this might take a week or so. In the meantime I will speak to your tutor and to the careers adviser. Have I got all that right?'

One advantage of summarizing is that it gives a sense of movement and purposefulness to the conversation. So when Sarah first begins to speak everything feels jumbled up and confused but by the end of 40 minutes she has some sense of perspective.

She also feels clearer about what the problems are and what she is going to do next. The teacher can say, 'So, we've looked at how you feel since your dog has died, and how it brings back memories of other losses that you've had; like your grandmother dying and how it was for you when you changed schools. I can see that you've had a lot of losses and have had to make quite a lot of changes. I'm wondering if you would find it helpful to meet again and allow yourself some time to talk a little more about these things?'

Summarizing at the end of the conversation does not mean that the issues have been tidied away, but it does mean that they have been defined so that they can be returned to at a later date. For some people the labelling of problems and feelings is helpful (for example, 'You've had a lot of losses'). This can in itself make a problem feel more manageable. Summarizing can also be especially helpful for students facing career decisions. It offers a way of seeing the total situation more clearly. The teacher may say, 'Phillip, you say you're not sure about what you want to do next. You've thought about GNVQs and think you may be interested in the intermediate level course, but before you do that you'd like to learn more about the course itself. I have offered to get some details for you by the end of the week and you are going to speak to your Dad about staying on at school. Then we'll meet again next Monday; how does that sound to you?'

Focusing

Focusing is selective attention to one subject or to the speaker herself. It can be used when the speaker is repeating herself or is jumping from one subject to another or going into unnecessary detail, sometimes in a circular fashion. The teacher can say, 'You've told me quite a lot about how it is with your Mum and your Mum's partner, and you've said you visit your Dad regularly. I wonder if you could tell me a bit more about how you feel when you go and see your Dad', or, 'You've mentioned several things that are bothering you. Could you say which seems the most pressing?'

Focusing tends to reduce the student's confusion and leads to greater understanding. If the teacher is feeling confused then this can be an important clue as to how the student feels herself. Care needs to be taken to keep the speaker focused but without being too authoritative. Tone of voice and manner are as important as the words used.

Sometimes it is difficult to select one aspect from everything that has been said. When Jane says, 'The Christmas holidays were awful. Everything went wrong. My parents rowed most of the time. I split up with my boyfriend and my friends were either busy working or with their families. On top of all that I was ill and had to miss a New Year's Eve party I'd really been looking forward to', the teacher can pick up one aspect. She can say, 'Your parents rowed most of the time?', or, 'You split up with your boyfriend?', or, 'You were ill?', or even, 'Your friends were busy?' In this instance, it is simpler to focus on the predominant feeling. The teacher can say, 'It sounds like the last two weeks have been very difficult and upsetting for you. I wonder if it would be helpful to look at what upsets you most?' The teacher can, of course, select one topic and ask, for example, more about the parents, but from what Jane has been saying it is not really clear which incident is bothering her most. The overriding feeling she describes is feeling 'awful'.

Sometimes a student goes off at a tangent about one of her friends. Here it is important to keep the student in focus, not her friend. For instance, Anne-Marie says of one of her friends, 'She only weighs six and a half stone and has got a really flat stomach. She's thin, she's pretty, she's popular and she's clever. She only eats once all day.' It is tempting to enquire about the friend, who it is, whether there is a problem, if the GP is involved or if her parents are aware. But it is important to keep the focus on Anne-Marie. It sounds as if Anne-Marie has been comparing herself unfavourably with her friend, and is likely to feel she is not good enough as she is. Any response should attempt to put the focus back to Anne-Marie. 'It sounds as if you compare yourself with your friend – and compare yourself unfavourably. Is that so?' The aim is to encourage Anne-Marie to talk more about herself even though it may be painful to do so. She may deflect attention from herself to her friend but if the teacher also switches her attention to the friend, Anne-Marie could easily think the teacher finds her friend more interesting than her.

Clarifying

Clarifying helps to bring vague material into sharper focus. It can be used to clear up confusion, but it needs to be used sparingly, since it can disrupt the flow of dialogue. For example, if Helen says, 'My Mum and my sister are always doing things together and I'm on my own a lot. She says I'm selfish and don't think about anyone else', it is not clear who 'she' refers to but it is relevant. The teacher may enquire, 'She? Your mother or your sister?' At times it is helpful to say, 'I'm not quite sure I followed that last part about what happened when your parents came home. Could you go over it again, please?'

Adolescents often speak in global terms about 'everyone else's parents', 'no-one', 'all teachers'. It is better not to correct the student, but to clarify exactly what is meant. The problem can then be looked at more accurately. 'Hayley, you say you're fed up with your teachers and that no one seems to care. I'm wondering if you really do mean everyone?' Hayley may reply, 'Well, yes and no. Most of the teachers can be okay, but it's just the Chemistry and Maths teachers that don't seem to care or notice you.'

The skill in asking for clarification is in putting it in terms of the teacher's confusion rather than the student's. If the teacher says, 'I didn't understand a word of what you just said', the student will feel criticized and will be reluctant to repeat herself. It is much better to say, 'There were so many things you were telling me there, that I got a bit confused. Would you mind telling me again what was said at the clinic?'

Using confrontation

Most people prefer to be liked than disliked, but there are times when a teacher needs to confront a student about punctuality, homework or behaviour, and for a time that teacher may become unpopular. Similarly in pastoral work there are times when painful issues have to be addressed, and if a teacher needs approval it may not be possible for her to confront issues. This will be to the detriment of the student.

When a teacher needs to draw attention to some undesirable behaviour or unrealistic attitude, the prospect of confronting

it can cause anxiety. The two extreme approaches are, colloqui-
ally, 'pussy footing' or 'taking a sledgehammer to crack a nut'.
There are two common fears behind confrontation: that the
person confronting will become a bad figure or will hurt the
feelings of the one who is confronted. There are risks involved in
using this approach and this skill requires a great deal of practice
to be used effectively. Confrontation has to be delivered in a
way which ensures it will be heard and not rejected outright, or
responded to defensively. Confrontation can alienate a student
and needs to be used advisedly. In effect the teacher is asking a
student to look at her own behaviour or her own shortcomings.
If this is badly handled the result can be withdrawal or silence,
or angry, defensive justification of the student's position.

By being confrontational a person is faced with the reality
of what she is saying or doing. At its simplest this can highlight
discrepancies between what is being said and what is being conveyed non-verbally. 'You say you get on okay with your friends,
but I sense in your manner and voice that maybe things are not
okay for you.' However, it is much more challenging to draw
attention to facts that the teacher knows the student will find
difficult to hear. 'On the one hand you say you want to have
a good career and go to college but on the other hand you don't
go to lessons or do the homework. Perhaps we can look at that.
You tell me how you see the situation.' The phrase, 'On the one
hand' is particularly useful when highlighting discrepancies or
incongruities. A teacher may feel tempted to say, 'Dean, how on
earth do you expect to get a college place if you don't do any
work?' Here her frustration is too evident. Were the teacher to
voice such sentiments Dean would be unlikely to think the teacher
either cares or is understanding.

Sometimes confronting does not immediately take effect.
Dean may come back to the teacher and say, 'I was lying in bed
last night thinking about what you said and I'm thinking that
maybe you have got a point. I do talk too much in lessons and
mess about and in the end it's me who suffers not the others. I
do want to make something of my life.'

A different and somewhat more positively charged confrontation is when someone holds a belief about themselves
which the teacher suspects is inaccurate. If the student suffers
from low self-esteem she may believe she is not liked, or is not

attractive, even if the reality is quite different. Reassurance rarely works. A teacher saying 'You are attractive', or 'People do like you' is likely to be rebuffed. If Anne Marie's self-esteem is low, it will be difficult to convince her because she will suspect the teacher is just being 'nice' or 'kind' to her. It can be more effective to say, 'You say that you aren't attractive and yet you've also told me you have had boyfriends', or, 'You say you aren't liked but yet you have got friends who you go around with and who invite you out.'

When a student holds unrealistic beliefs about herself, confrontation needs to be gentle. For instance, Simon may say he wants to go to university, but the teacher believes this to be extremely unlikely. It is not helpful to say, 'Simon, I'm afraid you've got no chance of getting into university', or, 'There's no way you can get a place at university based on your present performance.' Here the teacher appears to be giving vent to irritation or exasperation with Simon for not getting down to work earlier, and it does not help Simon to focus on himself more realistically. It is better to say, 'You say you would like to get to university, but I'm not sure you know what is required to get there and what this will mean for you. I'm wondering if we need to look at that together and also explore other possibilities that you may not have thought about – like GNVQs.'

It is important to frame confrontations in a calm yet assertive way. The point needs to be made clearly and succinctly, 'You say you hate your Saturday job, the boss, the people you work with, the travelling, but I wonder what it is that keeps you there rather than looking for a new job?' This is likely to be more effective than saying, 'Why on earth don't you get a better job', or, 'Stop moaning and do something about it then.' In these latter examples the teacher is responding to facts, but is not trying to understand what keeps Graham in the current job. It might transpire that his mother got him the job, and although he hates it, he does not want to upset her since she went to a lot of trouble to get him the work.

Again it is the tone of voice and manner in which responses are made that is crucial. In another situation, Sanjay says he really wants to do his work experience in an architects' office. He is really keen, and sure he will enjoy the work but despite being given a list of offices, he fails to make contact. The teacher feels frustrated and irritated by his inactivity and cannot understand his attitude. The teacher may feel tempted to say, 'Look Sanjay, I thought you really wanted this work and yet you've done nothing about it. Don't you realize you've got to get yourself organized, and get on to those architects' offices, or there won't be any places left; others will have got there before you? I can't spend any more time helping you if you don't help yourself.' This mini lecture may be satisfying for the teacher but it does not really address Sanjay's problem. He will just feel criticized. Instead the teacher might say, 'Sanjay, you tell me you're really keen to have your work experience in an architects' office, but I see that time is running out and you haven't been in contact with any of the firms. I'm wondering if something is holding you back or stopping you from getting this sorted out?' By saying this the teacher draws attention to the situation in an unemotional way and makes it possible to explore the problem further. It may be that Sanjay needs help writing a letter, or is worried about being away from home for long hours, because his mother relies on him to do the shopping or to collect the younger children from school.

Some self-defeating patterns of behaviour can take the form of 'games', similar to those described by Eric Berne (1966) in *Games People Play*. Some students ask for help but to every suggestion the reply comes, 'Well, yes, I've tried that but it doesn't work.' The important point here is to recognize that there is a pattern to such behaviour. Rather than collude with it, the pattern needs to be confronted, so that change becomes possible. As Adler is reported to have said, 'One of the most effective therapeutic means of challenging clients' games is "spitting in the patient's soup". The patient can continue with what he's doing but it no longer tastes so good.'

Students sometimes get into games about getting extra help or getting extensions. The 'hook' for the teacher is to be helpful, and the student can seem very appreciative, but it may be counterproductive in the long term. Some students also play the game of playing one teacher off against another. A student may say, 'Thank you for helping me. The other teachers never help me. They don't explain anything and I get so behind.' If there is a coercive feel to the request for help, or the teacher feels in some way that she is being manipulated, such behaviour can be

challenged calmly. The teacher can say, 'I have given you extensions for your work in the past, but I am beginning to wonder if
this really doesn't help you in the long term', or, 'I am glad to be
able to help you with your project but I wonder if there are any
useful lessons to be learned for the future.'

In any situation in which certain behaviour has to be
challenged, it is important to keep to the point and to suppress
the emotional dynamic. A teacher may feel like being angry, but
knows it will be inappropriate or unhelpful to express this openly.
Instead of saying, 'Come off it, Dean, that's a flimsy excuse. You
hardly ever give your work in on time', it is more constructive
to say, 'Well Dean, I've heard what you say about not being able
to give in your work, but I'm wondering how those reasons
sound to you?'

Giving information and answering questions

Teachers are skilled at passing on information, but an important distinction needs to be made between giving information and
giving advice. Advice is frequently sought but is not always wanted
or needed. Information needs to be specific and accurate, and
certain agencies offer specific information, for example the
Family Planning Association or the Citizens Advice Bureaux. Some
help may involve passing on the phone number of a helpline,
but advice as to what to do is usually inappropriate.

Sometimes problems are both emotional and practical.
In Hayley's case, she may need specific information and advice
from the health clinic about the 'morning-after' pill because
she had unprotected intercourse last night. However, Sophie's
decision as to whether or not to have a sexual relationship with
her boyfriend is also an emotional one. Contraceptive advice
may come into the discussion later, but the starting point is her
moral dilemma. When she has decided she is ready for a sexual
relationship, she will then need time and information to help
choose a suitable method of contraception. The teacher may feel
she should not embark on a sexual relationship, and may want
to give her the advice to 'wait' but the teacher's task is to help
Sophie make an informed decision, not impose a decision on
her. Sophie is obviously in two minds. It may be her boyfriend
is putting pressure on her; or she may really feel she's ready, but

knows her parents would be furious; or she knows a lot of her friends have lost their virginity, and she is curious to find out what sex is like. It will be more helpful to Sophie to explore her dilemma rather than to be given advice (see confidentiality in Chapter 6).

On the other hand informed opinion can be helpful if it is given by a trusted person with a sound knowledge of the issue. The danger in giving advice is that if it does not help, the student can rightly criticize the teacher or if a student does not take such advice, then she may feel reluctant to come back to talk further. Even if the advice proves to be good, dependency can be fostered and the student is not helped to acquire decision-making skills. It is important for students to learn to take responsibility for themselves and their actions.

There is of course a temptation, when Tina says, 'What would you do, Miss?', to accede to this request. The student is clearly expressing anxiety about making a decision, and wants to be dependent on the teacher's opinion. The skill here is to identify the issue, and to put this back to the student. 'You are asking me what I would do if I were in your shoes and thinking I was pregnant. I'm wondering if it would be more useful to look at what you feel about being pregnant and for us to talk about the options you have considered.'

If the teacher replies, 'If I were you I would . . .' this only reflects her own values. It does not actually help Tina think for herself. Making such a decision can be very difficult, but it is vital that it is Tina who makes it, since she will have to live with it for the rest of her life. It is no good just doing what her boyfriend, her parents, his parents, her friends want, even though she may take into account others' opinions. A teacher can help her sort out her own views from others' pressures. Similarly if Sophie asks, 'What method of contraception would you use?', the question can be answered: 'Perhaps you can tell me what methods you know about and which ones you might be interested in?' In any case it is inappropriate to be drawn into revealing the details of the teacher's personal or medical history.

There are two further points about advice giving that are relevant. First, in some cultures, it may be more acceptable to ask for advice or to take advice than to accept counselling. This is because advice is seen as more empowering. Second, some writers suggest that advice giving fulfils important needs in the advice giver, and in giving advice the giver demonstrates their superiority.

It is of course important to be well informed about the resources that are available in the community as well as in school, for example the school nurse, educational welfare officer, school counsellor, voluntary agencies, national helplines (see the list of useful organizations and addresses on page 116). A teacher has to be wary about offering even this information unless it has been clearly requested, or is definitely going to provide the type of information which the student appears to need.

The basic values underpinning counselling and the use of counselling skills are 'integrity, impartiality, and respect' (BAC 1998: A, 1999: C.1). In practice this means that anyone using counselling skills needs to convey their fundamental beliefs and values by attitude, manner and behaviour. If they are to create a safe environment in which students can explore feelings, thoughts and behaviour, teachers need to convey a warm response, and be supportive, reliable, trustworthy, consistent, non-judgmental, accepting and respectful of others.

While teachers can be more effective in their listening and responding skills they also need to give careful thought to the nature of the professional relationship, and how the right helping environment can be created in a school. So before teachers begin to apply these counselling skills they need to:

1 think about the physical environment i.e. the room, the type of chairs, the seating arrangements, privacy
2 be aware of the limits of confidentiality
3 be aware of their own level of competence; recognize the need for training and support and be able to refer appropriately in and out of school
4 be aware of their own prejudice, stereotyping, bias

These points are developed in Chapter 4.
Some dos and don'ts

Do:

1 Allow adequate time.
2 Put aside other worries and concerns.

3 Stay calm and relaxed.
4 Sit in a comfortable position paying attention to body posture.
5 Monitor tone and volume of voice.
6 Pay attention to non-verbal communication.
7 Engage in intermittent eye contact.
8 Allow pauses and brief silences.
9 Listen for underlying feelings.
10 Listen to oneself.
11 Be clear about the purpose of the meeting.
12 Remember details, names.
13 Demonstrate empathic understanding.
14 Help students explore feelings, at their own pace.
15 Ask open questions, unless specific information is needed.
16 Use simple language appropriate to the students' understanding.
17 Keep comments brief and to the point.
18 Only use confronting skills when the relationship is established.
19 Encourage students to find their own solutions.
20 Use minimal prompts.
21 Reflect feelings.
22 Paraphrase.
23 Summarize.
24 Clarify.
25 Listen.

Don't:

1 Make promises.
2 Promise confidentiality when it cannot be offered.
3 Be unreliable or forget appointments.
4 Flatter.
5 Stereotype, moralize, judge, criticize, blame, coerce, threaten,
ridicule or persuade.
6 Be dismissive, minimize or trivialize.
7 Reject.
8 Argue or contradict.
9 Show disbelief.
10 Make sarcastic remarks.
11 Interrupt.

12 Offer solutions.
13 Give advice.
14 Offer platitudes.
15 Talk too much.
16 Make loaded remarks.
17 Burden the student with personal details.
18 Ask a lot of questions.
19 Use 'should' or 'ought'.
20 Rush the ending.
21 Unnecessarily fill the silences.

Putting it together

Having learned various listening and responding skills, how might these come together in a conversation with a student? It is better if the teacher has access to a quiet room, free from interruption and distractions. The teacher needs to compose herself and put aside other worries and concerns for the duration of the meeting. In her own mind she needs to be clear about the limits of confidentiality, her level of competence, the purpose of the meeting, and the time that is available. It is not usually necessary to introduce the issue of confidentiality but if a student does so, her concerns can be discussed there and then (see professional boundaries and confidentiality in Chapters 4 and 6).

It is also helpful to say how much time is available. This has many advantages. First, the teacher does not feel under pressure to get to the problem immediately. Second, the student is able to pace herself and have some control over what is said and when. Third, the student feels valued knowing she has this time available to look at her problem. Lastly, with the pressure of time removed, both parties can relax a little; the teacher can settle to listening and a student can use the time to explore her problem. It is not right to allow someone to begin to talk about their problems without mentioning the time available, and then suddenly saying the time is up. The student may not have got round to mentioning the main concern. She also needs time to wind down which an abrupt ending does not permit.

Pastoral work can spread over free periods, lunch breaks, and the ends of the day, and the net result is that the teacher feels there is very little space for her to reflect and think. She can feel drained and tired (see support in Chapter 4). It is good practice to set aside a particular period of time for pastoral work, and to be clear about the time available for any one student. The teacher also needs to be mindful about the number of students she can see in the week.

At the beginning of a meeting some students may need some help to start. Nervousness at such times is to be expected and is quite normal. A simple comment can help to put the student at ease and encourage her to start talking. For example, 'Perhaps you can tell me what has been bothering you', or, 'I guess it is hard to know where to start. I am happy for you to start wherever you want', or, 'Perhaps you feel a bit anxious about coming to see me. If I just sit and listen and let you talk, will that be all right?' It is not necessary to begin with small talk about the weather, summer holidays, or a football game. This takes valuable time away from the purpose of the meeting. Moreover it highlights the awkwardness of the teacher who is unable to move straight into the student's concerns.

If a student is invited to talk freely rather than be subjected to a barrage of questions she is much more likely to open up about what is troubling her. The teacher says in her manner, her body language, and her tone of voice, 'Over to you, the time is yours.' After the teacher has recognized and acknowledged the initial nervousness or hesitation the student may then be able to relax into the meeting. The pacing of the meeting needs careful monitoring, so that important issues are not rushed at the end. Cameron (1963: 769) makes the following point about therapists, but it also applies to teachers, 'Like the good gardener [he] waits until he recognizes something which is struggling to emerge and then makes it easier for it to emerge.'

It is important for the teacher to accept the student's pace, so that the student feels safe enough to explore her feelings, which cannot in any case be rushed. Sometimes it can be helpful to let a student pour out her feelings and in subsequent meetings to focus on one problem at a time. At other times, the teacher may have to discourage the student from giving excessive detail. She may say, 'You have said quite a lot about how it is for you at home, but let's look at some of those things one by one', or, 'There is a lot going on for you at the moment. I think it will be helpful if we just look at one thing at a time. Is that all right by you?'

As the end of the meeting approaches, the teacher might remind the student, 'We've got about five minutes left.' This enables the teacher to summarize, make arrangements, and check with the student on what they have agreed. It also prepares the student so that she does not feel hurried out of the room or rejected. Similarly, if she has been crying it allows her a few minutes to compose herself before going to a lesson. Because the time available was made clear at the beginning, the teacher is not pushed into giving more time at the end if the student did not get round to talking about all the problems. If there is not going to be sufficient time the teacher can acknowledge this and say, 'I am aware that we have only got a few minutes left and we have hardly scratched the surface of things that are bothering you. Rather than rush now, do you think it will be helpful for us to meet again?'

Some people introduce important or new issues just as a conversation is coming to an end. In everyone's interest it is better to acknowledge the importance of this new subject, but stay firm that another time needs to be found to discuss it. Once a time boundary has been extended it can be difficult to re-establish.

In the last five to ten minutes a student can be asked whether it has been helpful to talk, and whether or not she would like to meet again. Some students welcome the opportunity, while others prefer to think about whether or not they want a further meeting. The object of such a question is not to elicit appreciation or gratitude, but to establish whether the student finds the process helpful. It also allows the student power and control over their situation. Not all students want to discuss their feelings and problems, and if this is so their wishes must be respected.

At the end of a meeting it may be obvious that the problem is going to be long term, and therefore helpful to offer the student an informal 'contract' or verbal agreement. The teacher may say, 'From what you have told me I am wondering whether it might be helpful to meet each week from now until half term and then review how things are. It seems that while your Mum is in hospital you may want some time to talk about how things are going. What do you think?'

A suggestion of meeting once a week for a few weeks can be very comforting and 'holding' for someone who is going through a difficult period. Knowing a teacher is willing to give a regular time can help a student feel cared for. Alternatively, knowing that support is available can mean that while a student does not have to take it up, she feels better because it has been offered. By offering a regular time the teacher's own timetable can be better managed. In this respect it is worth considering which times in the day can be used for regular and which for urgent requests.

Summary

In any meeting of this kind there is always an element of 'not knowing'. The teacher will not 'know' what the student is going to say, and cannot really prepare for whatever will emerge. However, if she remembers her listening skills and tries to relax, listen attentively, and not rehearse her responses, she will be able to help the student explore her concerns. Each person will find their own style, but if teachers remember and practise these basic listening and responding skills, and so tune into the student, the student will feel valued and respected. Inevitably some of the feelings expressed by the student may be difficult and painful to hear, but if the teacher can 'contain' those feelings, and hold them safe, eventually many students will be able to make sense of them. Good listening and responding is sometimes straightforward, but sometimes it can be a difficult task. With some students it can be tiring and demanding, but it is, nevertheless, a very worthwhile part of the teacher's pastoral role.

Chapter 4

Implications of using counselling skills

One of the purposes of the teacher using counselling skills is to enable a student to 'recognize feelings, thoughts and behaviours and, when appropriate, to explore them in greater depth' (BAC 1999: C.5). This means giving a student the opportunity to face and explore feelings without fear or criticism. It is not enough to say simply, 'Go ahead'. She has to feel she can trust the teacher and that it is safe enough to do so. This safety is achieved by providing clear 'boundaries'. These boundaries refer to professional, physical and personal boundaries.

For this kind of work to take place it must be in a relationship, of which a fundamental component is trust. Trust takes time to develop, and varies very much between students. Young people who have had trustworthy figures in their lives are much more likely to trust teachers than those who have been let down or betrayed by significant adults. This is particularly so with students who have been abused. Such students may prove more difficult to help because they cannot trust easily and need to test the teacher's reliability and dependability.

Using counselling skills involves giving students time and space to understand and clarify their problems, and to make meaningful choices where they can arrive at their own conclusions rather than being told what to do. This is a simple enough statement to make but in practice it is a complex process. The listener has to be patient while the student struggles with her problems. The solution may appear obvious to the teacher, but it is vital that a student finds her own answers. The skill of the helper is to create the right environment to facilitate this process.

It is very reassuring for a student to have her fears taken seriously and explored especially when they cannot be easily removed. For instance, if a student's mother is in hospital undergoing a biopsy, it is more helpful to talk about her worst fears of her mother dying or having cancer than rush in with reassurances that everything will be all right. If a student feels the teacher can tolerate fears and worries, this in itself can be very comforting. There are no easy answers in life and if a student learns that a trusted adult can tolerate uncertainties, this is in itself helpful. The important point about listening to a student's worries is to listen and not dismiss them, however irrational they may seem. Feelings do not go away by being dismissed, they just go into hiding. Only by exploring worries do they lessen in intensity and feel more manageable.

At times the teacher may feel frustrated and helpless and may want to 'do' something. The feeling of helplessness, particularly in the face of terminal illness, death or disaster, is very real and can be quite overwhelming. If the teacher can try and stay with such feelings and be confident in just 'being' with a student, rather than 'doing something', she will perform a good service. Just to sit and 'be' with someone, even when they are experiencing great sadness or despair, helps the other person realize that their feelings are normal and can be survived.

Boundaries

This term is commonly referred to in counselling literature. It is important since it emphasizes the safety of setting limits. Parents and teachers know that children test boundaries, especially adolescents. All children need firm boundaries to buck against and to know they will still be in place. This creates a feeling of safety. So it is in counselling where the aim is to create a safe environment. If students have no limits, no boundaries, despite the initial cry of excitement they feel bewildered and lost. The way a safe, trusting environment can be created is by establishing firm professional and personal boundaries. These will be considered in turn.

Professional boundaries

There are limits of a teacher's role, limits to confidentiality and to legal responsibilities. Since confidentiality is discussed in a later chapter (see Chapter 6) only a few brief points need to be made here. Where a teacher is clear about the limits of confidentiality she will feel more confident in her role. In most day-to-day encounters with students, the issue does not arise. However, it is important for the teacher to develop a sense of when a student is beginning to talk about matters which the student may regard as confidential but which might compromise the teacher. At such times it is better to interrupt a student than allow her to continue and for her then to say, 'But you won't tell anyone, will you?' The teacher can interrupt and say, 'I'm wondering if it would be helpful here for me to explain that usually what any student talks to me about is confidential; but there are exceptions and so I want you to know that there may be circumstances when I would have to speak to the head teacher.' This will of course interrupt the flow of the conversation, but it is better for a student to make an informed decision as to whether or not to continue. In many instances, a student will preface her talk with a question about confidentiality. For instance she may say, 'Is everything I say to you private?', or, 'If I tell you something, will you have to talk to my parents?' This is the time to explore the question of confidentiality. Promises cannot be given even if a student begins, 'Promise you won't tell anyone?' One response is to say, 'I can't make promises, but if I have to speak to anyone about what we are talking about, I will tell you first' (see disclosures in Chapters 5 and 6).

Promises cannot be made in advance of disclosure or about practical arrangements. For instance, if a student says, 'You will promise to see me then, won't you?', a teacher needs to be clear about her intentions. She can say, 'I can't promise to see you, but what I will do is arrange to see you at a specific time. If, for any reason, I can't be with you, I'll make sure you get a message.' In making such a request, a student might be revealing that she has had experiences of people letting her down, and it is difficult for her to trust. It is important for teachers to be dependable and reliable.

With regard to the teacher's availability there may be times during the school day when a student wishes to talk to a teacher when it is genuinely inconvenient. To maintain good personal boundaries the teacher can offer to see the student briefly before registration or at the end of the day. Knowing that a teacher is there, and can then make time later in the day, provides some security and stability especially in a crisis.

Colleagues

Information about a student should not be passed on to colleagues unless it is in the student's interests. Doing so can be construed as 'gossiping' by the student, and is likely to damage her trust in the staff. It is inappropriate when Mrs Carter says, 'I hear from Miss Daniels that . . .', because if Miss Daniels needs to talk to Mrs Carter, she needs to check this with the student first. Teachers hear a lot about students in the staff room, but a teacher needs to be clear about what she has heard or overheard in general conversation, and what she has been told in her professional capacity.

It is also important when a student talks about a particular teacher not to get drawn into discussing the personality of that teacher or to share personal observations, however tempting it may be. It is not professional to say, 'Oh I know what you mean about Mr Taylor. He does go on, doesn't he?' It is more helpful to ascertain the student's experience. The teacher can say, 'What is it about your science lessons that makes it difficult for you to settle down and work?' It is important not to take sides, to gossip or to allow students to play one teacher off against another.

Role conflict

Since a teacher has several roles, educative, administrative, evaluative, authoritative and vocational, there is always potential for role conflict. This may be particularly so for a year head who carries an obvious disciplinary function alongside her pastoral duties. In practice, this means that a teacher may need to mark work; to write reports and references; to speak to parents; to organize transitions between schools; to investigate complaints; to answer queries; to discipline; to organize and take part in extra-curricular activities; and to listen to worried or distressed students. One deputy head teacher, Anne Jones (1984), found she could not effectively combine her roles of deputy head and counsellor, whereas Alick Holden (1971) claimed he could. Much will depend on the ethos of the school, the overall continuum of pastoral care, the allocation of time and the level of support. Steps towards minimizing role conflict can be taken, such as being clear about each different role and the limits of responsibility in each. Clear policy guidelines will help both teacher and student to be clear about accountability and responsibility.

Taking sides

When a teacher uses her counselling skills with a small group of students, for example when dealing with bullying, she needs to pay attention to each student equally, otherwise one student can feel marginalized and may not accept the conclusion of the discussion. Children are very keen that things are 'fair' and even though they may not like the outcome, they will often accept a decision as long as it feels fair. A teacher has to suspend her opinion about who did what, until she has heard everybody speak. This is equally important when a teacher meets with parents. It is not a matter of taking the side of the parent or the student, but of listening carefully to both sides. This is particularly difficult when the teacher hears racist, sexist, or ageist arguments, but she can sometimes use reflecting, paraphrasing and summarizing skills to good effect at such times.

Parents

For a teacher to be clear about her responsibilities towards parents this needs to be made clear in the school policy guidelines. If a teacher becomes aware that a parent would welcome and benefit from counselling, it is not her responsibility to extend pastoral work to the parent. If a parent's crisis has an effect on a student, the teacher needs to be clear about her boundaries, and not be drawn into extended phone calls or interviews with the parent. It is better tactfully to suggest contacting the GP, Relate or a counselling centre.

It is also important that a teacher is clear about the purpose of any meeting with a parent. She has to consider whether or not it is appropriate for the student to be part of it. Much depends on the nature of the concern, but it is usually helpful to explain to the student the purpose of the meeting, whether or not she is invited to attend. This raises issues of trust where it is important that communication is clear. Once trust has been broken it is difficult to re-establish.

If the teacher has to make a home visit there can be practical difficulties. The most usual distractions are the television or radio, pets and younger children. It is better to arrange to call at an agreed time, rather than interrupt a favourite television programme or to arrive at a meal time. If the television or radio is on it is unreasonable to expect to discuss matters. The teacher might say, 'I can stay for half an hour, because there are several matters I'd like to discuss. I'd find it helpful if the television could be turned off, since I know I'll find it distracting', or, 'Would you mind if the radio is turned off? I'm sure we'll concentrate better on what we need to talk about.' Where there are pets and young children tact is again required and such situations might mean the necessity of using the skill of confrontation.

Consideration has to be given to the possibility that a parent may not speak English, or that English is the second language. It has been the practice in some schools to use the student as interpreter, but this practice is now discouraged since it places an unreasonable demand on the student, and the translation may not be reliable. Sometimes another relative or member of staff can be called upon to translate, but thought should be given to compiling a list of local people who are able to offer translating services. Inevitably the discussion is distorted by the presence of a third party, and by the process of relaying thoughts, feelings and opinions through an interpreter but this is perhaps preferable to using the student herself.

Power and authority

A teacher has considerable power over a student, and even if she chooses not to exercise it, the student is aware of the potential. It can be difficult for some students to trust a teacher, partly because of their life experiences, but also because of this power imbalance. Even if the teacher feels comfortable about the disparity in age, status and power, the student may not be comfortable. This can of course be different for a newly qualified teacher who lacks confidence in her role, and is unsure about procedures within school, but it is an important dynamic that can easily be overlooked.

Students can feel vulnerable when talking about personal problems and the teacher needs to respect any information she is given. She should not discuss personal information with other teachers or the student's parents without her permission. Moreover any such information should never be used when disciplinary action is being considered. The inherent power imbalance, role conflict as well as the potential for exploitation is recognized by the BAC in their *Code of Ethics and Practice Guidelines for Those Using Counselling Skills in their Work* (BAC 1999). The teacher is recommended to consult this code.

Practical arrangements

The room

Wherever possible it is important to have a quiet undisturbed room available for seeing students or parents. Rooms are always at a high premium in schools, but given that teachers are expected to interview parents and students, governors and senior management need to address the requirement for interview rooms. The room does not have to be large or lavishly furnished. Ideally there should be space for two or three comfortable chairs of the same type. A coffee table and a small lamp can help to create an informal, relaxed atmosphere. A box of tissues is also helpful, as is a clock. There is no need to provide tea and coffee making facilities. The room should be of a comfortable temperature. The siting is also important since a lot of noise can be distracting. Consideration might need to be given to soundproofing.

The provision of a quiet room conveys the message to parents and students that private meetings and discussions matter. Parents and students feel valued, and it reduces the level of stress for the teacher if she is able to work under favourable conditions. Some schools set aside one or two rooms that can be booked for interviews. If a year office has to be used, some thought can be given to dividing the room into a work and a seating area. Much depends on the imagination of the teacher and the conditions in the school. Similarly, attention has to be paid to signs on the door, 'Engaged' or 'Free'. Some teachers use the convention of leaving a door open if they are free and closing the door if they are busy or engaged. Problems can arise if several people use the office, but again representation can be made to the head teacher and the governing body about appropriate facilities.

The real hindrances to good interviews are not so much poor facilities as interruptions, which cause both the teacher and the student to lose concentration. It is very disheartening to have to say to the student, 'Now, where were we?' With some forethought some interruptions can be avoided or minimized, such as signs on doors or telephones being diverted. Interruptions not only interfere with the flow of discussion but also interfere with the teacher's listening. If she takes a telephone call, no matter how brief, there is a risk that the student will feel she is imposing on the teacher's time when she needs to attend to another person. In the long run it is better to give undivided attention to a student for half an hour than to have a longer meeting made messy because of the interruptions.

It is not advisable for a teacher to offer individual counselling to a student either in the teacher's own home or in the student's home. This blurs the line between a professional relationship and a friendship.

Length of meetings

It is good if a teacher is clear about the time available for a meeting and this helps the teacher manage her time better so that she is less likely to feel stressed. A meeting of between 15 and 30 minutes can be set aside as it is unlikely that more than 30 minutes will be needed. If there is more to discuss further meetings can be offered. Occasionally longer meetings may be indicated but these should not exceed 50 minutes. Under certain circumstances an informal 'contract' can be offered, particularly during periods of crisis. For instance, the teacher may suggest meeting once a week for an agreed time, for four to six weeks.

If it becomes clear that insufficient time is available to deal with the student's concerns it is better to offer another occasion, rather than extend the agreed time. If the time is extended it puts pressure on the teacher and also weakens the security of the time boundary. A teacher can indicate, 'We only have ten minutes left. I realize we can't do justice to your concerns in that time, so perhaps we need to meet again?' If a student takes time to settle to talk the teacher may need to consider whether she allowed too much time for general chat and did not use her focusing skills enough.

Ending a meeting can be difficult for both student and teacher. If a student is seen on a regular basis and always seems to want more than the agreed time, it can be helpful to discuss this. It might be better to meet for longer, and less often, or for shorter periods more often. The teacher can say, 'I'm struck by the fact that we keep running out of time. We only seem to talk about what's really bothering you after a quarter of an hour or so.' It is sometimes necessary to give permission to the student to launch straight away into the problem. Perhaps the student thought she had to be polite and make general conversation first.

One feature of ending formal counselling sessions is what Bierkens (cited in Lang and van der Molen 1990: 133) calls the 'door handle phenomenon', and this also happens in informal counselling. Here the student begins to talk about a problem just as she is leaving. In these situations it is better to acknowledge that an important topic has been mentioned but there is not enough time available to discuss it properly. 'What you have just mentioned sounds important but unfortunately we've come to the end of our agreed time. I wonder if you'd like to arrange another time to meet and then we can talk about it properly?' It may be frustrating and somewhat tantalizing to be given a snippet of information, but it is important not to be pushed into extending the time. Of course there are exceptions, but as a rule, it is good practice to keep to the time agreed.

If a teacher has been seeing a student regularly, thought needs to be given to 'weaning off' the process. This is best done in consultation with the student. Time may be needed for the student to readjust after a period of crisis. She is more likely to feel capable and confident about managing her problem if she feels the teacher is there in the background and willing to help if necessary, than if she feels suddenly rejected and abandoned.

Holidays

Consideration also needs to be given to the effect holidays have on some students in terms of taking away their main sources of support. If the teacher has been seeing the student regularly it might be necessary to discuss alternative lines of support several weeks before a holiday. Some students rely on friends, especially if support is lacking in the home, or turn to local organizations such as youth clubs or helplines. A particular worry can be the long summer holiday. Sometimes, if a teacher expects to go into school in the holidays, she can arrange to meet a student. A seven-week holiday can feel a long time for a student, although the offer to meet halfway through can be supportive. Such arrangements should be thought through, and be the exception rather than the rule.

Records

A teacher needs think about what information is put onto a student's school record, especially since some students may be sensitive about anything that could go into references or university applications. The legal position is that a young person, subject to certain exceptions, is entitled to apply for access to their school records at the age of 16. Parents may apply for access to the records of their children under the age of 16 (Regulations 4 (1) and 6 (1) Education (School Records) Regulations 1989) (DES 1989). For child protection records see access to records in Chapter 6.

Personal boundaries

This is a difficult area for some teachers, and consideration needs to be given to the type of relationship a teacher wants with a student, and how a teacher's personal and professional needs are met (see self-awareness later in this chapter). Teaching involves a professional relationship. It is not a friendship even if it is a relationship that is friendly. Friendship offers a two-way exchange, with sharing that comes about over time and based on trust and reliability. It may be one-sided in times of need, but essentially it is a mutual and equal relationship. To think of counselling or using counselling skills as indicative of a friendship is misleading. The qualities needed in a counselling relationship may be similar to those found in a good personal relationship, yet there is an important difference. A helper can feel deep satisfaction at being able to help, but this is not a mutual, helping relationship. Noonan (1983: vii) suggests, 'Counselling fills the space between psychotherapy and friendship.'

Teachers are usually very caring and can with the best of intentions give out their home address and their home telephone number, but this can give rise to problems. The information can be abused, with the teacher contacted in unsocial hours; or the frequency of calls may prove intrusive. A student may make contact when it is genuinely inconvenient for a teacher to deal with a problem, so that the teacher feels compromised and the student feels rejected. Once a boundary has been extended it can be difficult to re-establish the normal teacher–student relationship. For this reason support is best offered during the school day. If a situation merits additional help it may be necessary to involve other agencies (see making a referral in Chapter 5 and the list of organizations and addresses on page 116).

Use of first names

In some schools staff and students alike use first names and find this works satisfactorily. In most schools, however, teachers are referred to more formally by title. In a formal counselling context a counsellor sometimes uses first names, but in a school a teacher's primary role is that of teacher, so it is usual for a teacher to follow the school conventions. This formality also helps to maintain the professional boundary. It is less confusing to the student since she has contact with the same teacher in the execution of her other duties.

Touch

Generally speaking the controversy around the topic of touch centres not on formal greetings, such as a handshake, but on the question of whether or not it is appropriate to touch the student in other ways. One of the difficulties here is that what seems appropriate and reassuring to one person can feel intrusive to another. This is a particular concern if there has been a history of sexual abuse and since this may not be known at first, assumptions can never made about whether physical contact is either desirable or acceptable. Moreover, there are variations in these matters between cultures and between the sexes. In any society there are rules about who may be touched, by whom, on which part of the body, in what way, and on which occasions. For instance, if a student is crying because there has been a death in the family, it may seem natural for a teacher to put her arm around her shoulder, but not everyone welcomes close contact and the gesture may not be appreciated. For a male teacher to comfort a female student in such a way may be even less acceptable. It is possible to convey understanding and compassion without touching by empathic responses. The Department for Education and Employment guidelines 10/95 (DfEE 1995b) advise teachers to 'be sensitive to a child's reaction to physical contact and to act appropriately'. In respect of children with special education needs (SEN) the circular offers the following advice: 'Physical contact may be a necessary part of teaching some pupils with SEN, for example visually impaired children or those with profound or multiple learning difficulties. Schools with such pupils may wish to consider developing clear guidelines for staff which maintain a balance between providing support and preventing abuse.'

Self-awareness

A vital element in counselling skills training is the need to develop greater self-awareness, particularly of personal values, beliefs and prejudices. The helper needs to be open to different values, attitudes and experiences. It is important to be aware of personal motivation for the work and to recognize the helper's own physical and emotional needs.

Self-awareness is particularly relevant when working with students who are in some way different, by way of gender, race, age, ethnicity, sexual orientation, class, disability or economic status. Some awareness of others' lives and experience is gained by seeing television programmes or films, in travelling and by reading novels and poems; but an important dimension in personal awareness is that it comes from introspection and sharing perceptions with others. Helpful feedback can be gained from colleagues, family and friends informally and from participating in training days, workshops, experiential courses and role plays. Sharing feelings and thoughts with others and receiving feedback about personal abilities and limitations is vital, even if it involves taking some personal risks in self-disclosure.

Various situations test the teacher's basic values and beliefs and highlight differences between herself and others, such as abortion, adoption, divorce, criminal activity, use of drugs and suicide. At such times, it is important to be aware of the different beliefs held by others so that a teacher does not impose her own set of values on to a student. Some values are universally held, for example that killing human beings is wrong, but there is considerable variation in beliefs about a whole range of other issues. A teacher may believe it is better for parents to stay together 'for the sake of the children' or she may believe an unhappy marriage may be more damaging for the children than the parents' living apart. Such beliefs may be grounded in personal experience, religious teachings, public opinion or personal observations. It is important to recognize differences of opinion and belief, and that these may need to be explored rather than judged or criticized.

I have suggested above that some distraction in listening (see guidelines for listening in Chapter 2) comes from noises outside the room. There are other less obvious distractions in the room which bear consideration, such as a student's appearance and demeanour, or the teacher's anxieties, ill-health or personal preoccupations. If a student is personable, it may be easier for the teacher to listen to her concerns than to those of another student who is not. Alternatively, the teacher may find herself distracted from what the student is saying if the student's appearance is striking because of hairstyle, for example, or make-up, clothes, jewellery or tattoos. A teacher will probably find it easier to engage with a student who speaks clearly rather than one who mumbles or stutters, especially since the latter may be more difficult to follow and make for harder work on the part of the teacher. A teacher needs to be aware of the effect that each student has on her, and how she relates to that person.

There is also a risk of stereotyping certain students because of their appearance, gender, race, religion, disability or sexual orientation. The teacher may recognize difference but not fully understand the experiences and cultural norms of particular students. This has obvious relevance for a white teacher working with racial minority groups and a black teacher working in a predominantly white school. It is difficult to listen to anyone in a completely unbiased way. What usually happens is that information is 'screened' or 'filtered' according to the individual bias of a teacher, which may not be fully recognized. Hall (1977: 85) makes the point well: 'One of the functions of culture is to provide a highly selective screen between man and the outside world. In its many forms, culture therefore designates what we pay attention to and what we ignore.' What is important is that the teacher develops an awareness of her own cultural background and cultural norms, and is receptive to learning more about other cultures whether they appear similar or different to her own. Awareness is the first step towards breaking down prejudice and unhelpful bias.

Personal needs

A teacher's job is very demanding and counselling of any sort, though rewarding, can be very stressful. This is why it is important to think about how much time the teacher devotes to it. She has to take account of her priorities, where she places her efforts, as well as her personal resources. If the teacher is overstressed, then either ill-health or burn-out can result (see stress and burn-out later in this chapter).

The teacher and the school together need to look at how much time is allocated for pastoral work. Teachers have non-contact periods in their working week and often use this time to see students. Management can underestimate the time needed for pastoral work and exploit the goodwill of teachers. The teacher needs to monitor her personal resources as well as her personal suitability for the work. She needs to be firm about the time she gives to it. She may have to be flexible and respond to emergencies, but if she is not to be overloaded she has to set realistic boundaries.

She has to also work within the limits of her competence. If she is constantly reacting to demands not only will she become tired and drained, but may become resentful and less effective. A teacher who is clear about her role, her level of competence and the time set aside will be more effective than a teacher who tries to deal with every problem, even those for which she has not had enough training, and for which she does not have sufficient time (see levels of competence later in this chapter).

A teacher undertaking any counselling activity will feel better equipped to do so if she has had some basic training and has read some of the counselling literature. It is unreasonable to expect teachers to know how to counsel without this. Common sense is necessary but not sufficient and the skills that can be learned make the work more effective and manageable. Issues discussed in this and the next two chapters bear careful consideration if pitfalls are to be avoided. This is also a matter for senior management, so that funds are made available for training.

A more complicated and potentially fraught area for discussion are the emotional needs of the teacher. Self-awareness includes looking at personal motivation. While altruism is a questionable concept it is important that the teacher does not use students to meet her own emotional needs, or to escape from her own problems in school or outside it. If a teacher enjoys having students dependent on her it may be difficult for her to help students to become independent. She may, unconsciously, keep a student dependent to meet her own needs. Similarly, a teacher may take on a great deal of pastoral work because she likes to be needed. While it is reasonable to 'enjoy' pastoral work, the teacher has to consider whether or not it can become a substitute for other ways of living.

Many people in the helping professions have higher needs for nurturing than other people, and the question arises as to how those needs can best be met. The teacher may need to review her support system to see her needs are met appropriately. As Appell (1963: 148) says, 'The most significant resource a counselor brings to a helping relationship is himself. It is difficult to understand how a counselor unaware of his own emotional needs, of his expectations of himself as well as others, of his rights and privileges in relationships can be sensitive enough to such factors in his counselee.'

Another aspect to consider is the teacher's need for 'achievement'. If 'success' is the principal objective, 'success' needs to be defined. By whom and by what standard is it measured? Many students are helped but the 'evidence' is often invisible. Dramatic 'success' may not be feasible, and that objective can place a teacher under unrealistic pressure to perform miracles. The need for success may mean a teacher is selective about the students to whom she offers help. She may choose to work with bright, motivated students, and refer on the disaffected and less able students.

A further problem can arise if the teacher needs to be right, or needs to manage and organize others. It can be difficult for such teachers to allow students to express their feelings honestly, or to allow them time to develop trust so that they can explore issues in their own time, finding their own solutions.

Self-disclosure

There is much controversy about self-disclosure, that is, personal disclosures made by the helper to the person being helped. The intention of self-disclosure should always and only be to assist the other in self-exploration or self-understanding and has to be appropriate. It should encourage the person seeking help to talk more openly, or to feel more understanding of themselves. Self-disclosure can be misleading and unhelpful, with a student feeling burdened by what a teacher reveals more than feeling better as a result. Furthermore, a teacher may disclose details of her life experience which she cannot be sure will remain confidential (which may or may not matter). Students vary in their level of maturity, but no student can be automatically expected to hold such confidences or secrets.

For many reasons any self-disclosure needs to be selective, and not detract from the student's concerns. Some studies have shown that helper self-disclosure can frighten clients and make their helper seem less well-adjusted. There is the risk that self-disclosure shifts the focus from the student to the teacher. The question also arises as to what the teacher's motives are for making these disclosures. Schwartz and Abel (cited in Truax and Carkhuff 1967: 218) emphasize, 'The psychotherapist (does not) solve his own problems and seek fulfilment through the patient. The patient is permitted to try to solve his own problems in his own way, to gratify his own needs without having to satisfy those of the therapist.'

For these reasons it is not normally helpful to give detailed personal accounts such as, 'When I was in the sixth form, I remember my father wanting me to apply to Oxford to read history and my mother wanted me to live at home. We had so many arguments. I remember one really bad row when . . .'. A better way of conveying understanding is by making an empathic response (using such experiences) such as, 'When you're in the sixth form it can seem as if there are so many decisions to make.'

Stress and burn-out

People need a certain amount of stress in order to perform adequately in their daily life. However, if a person experiences too much stress, there are different consequences. These may be physical (migraine, headaches, feeling tired all the time); emotional (anger, denial, anxiety, depression); or behavioural (being late, eating too much or too little, sleeping too much or too little, inability to be alone, avoiding contact with others). Furthermore there may also be disruptions in thought processes (inability to think clearly, poor concentration, memory loss, indecision). All these consequences of stress are relevant to the teacher as well as the student.

The term burn-out is now commonly applied to personal situations where feelings are of being inadequate, helpless, tired, drained and without enthusiasm. Edelwich (1980) describes the four stages of disillusionment moving from enthusiasm to stagnation, frustration and apathy. Of the second stage Newman and Newman (1979: 430) write, 'The person loses sight of the potential for nurturing, educating or guiding others and becomes trapped in the struggle to protect or maintain the self.' Given this undesirable state steps need to be taken to recognize the condition.

Box 4.1: Possible causes of burn-out

Burn-out can result from:
- being under constant pressure to produce results within a set time
- work requiring a lot of energy over a long time
- performing tasks which are repeated over and over again
- a lack of trust between the individual and others
- working under difficult circumstances with difficult groups
- having unresolved personal conflicts, for example, health, marital problems
- being given unrealistic performance targets
- inadequate training for the task
- insufficient resources
- insufficient time
- no support or encouragement from colleagues or management
- being subject to criticism, humiliation, bullying at work
- no relaxation
- personal needs not being met
- giving large amounts of personal and emotional energy to others without results

---

While all these factors do not relate specifically to a teacher's pastoral work they are mentioned because a teacher may experience considerable stress in her teaching role, and by undertaking further emotionally demanding work the teacher may be at risk of suffering from burn-out. These pressures are familiar to teachers and the clustering of such pressures certainly can contribute to fatigue and burn-out.

However, there are ways of preventing this. One way is for the school and the individual to develop an awareness of these factors and for both to recognize that there are legitimate needs which should be met. In respect of any counselling work there is a need for appropriate training, professional support, supervision or consultation, appropriate facilities, adequate time, policy guidelines, and clear statements of accountability and responsibility. Besides this the individual teacher has to take responsibility for her own well-being and find time for reflection and relaxation, interests outside school, and her personal needs for love and friendship.

Levels of competence

The concept of levels of competence is valuable when applied to teachers undertaking pastoral work. There are many problems with which a teacher can deal, but there are certain problems that need to be referred either to a colleague or to another professional, for example, a counsellor, psychologist, or psychiatrist. The teacher needs to be clear about the limits of her responsibility and the extent of her knowledge and skills. This is one feature of her professionalism (see making a referral in Chapter 5). BAC emphasizes this point: 'Practitioners are responsible for working within the limits of their competence' (BAC 1999: C.4.2).

If a teacher is able to work within her level of competence she is less likely to feel stressed. She is much more likely to experience stress and fatigue if she is frequently battling to deal with problems for which she has had little or no training. It is better for her to make a referral to a specialist agency and then offer continuing support, rather than feel overwhelmed by a student's problems. They are usually able to discuss problems and give support. Learning and using counselling skills greatly helps a teacher deal with many problems such as bullying, relationship breakdowns, or bereavement.

However, problems do not come neatly packaged and labelled. There are many issues encountered by teachers in school for which particular help is needed, but community resources are often severely stretched and the waiting list is frequently long. Problems do not go away because they have been assessed as being serious and meriting specialist help. There is no simple answer to this complex issue of resources. There is an important question of where responsibility lies. Is the problem the student's, the parent's, the school's or the service provider's? At the end of the day a teacher sees a student in school and tries to offer what help she can.

So the teacher needs to recognize those problems for which she has responsibility and can work with effectively, and then work within the limits of her competence and with the time she has available. She cannot respond to all the problems in the school. She has neither the time nor the training nor the competence for every problem. If they extend beyond her competence, it may be necessary to raise the profile of pastoral work and discuss the issue with senior management and the governors. It may even be necessary to consider whether or not a counselling post is needed.

To summarize, a teacher can be helped to feel more confident and competent in her pastoral work if she is given clarification of her role, duties and responsibilities; adequate time; and clear policy guidelines (each school should have its own policy statements). It is also helpful to have clear systems of referral; specific information readily available (for example, on drugs); and details of statutory and voluntary agencies. Finally, appropriate training, support, access to consultation, and feedback on performance will all be helpful.

Training

The BAC *Code of Ethics and Practice Guidelines for Those Using Counselling Skills in their Work* recommends: 'Practitioners are responsible for ensuring that they have training in the use of counselling skills and that this training is appropriate and sufficient for the counselling skills work they undertake' (BAC 1999: C.4.1).

Training needs can be met at two levels. First, teachers can attend basic counselling skills courses, enrol on more advanced counselling certificate courses or attend modular courses at local colleges and university. They can also attend workshops on specialist issues, for example bullying, bereavement, and drug and alcohol abuse. Second, within the school itself speakers can be invited to provide training to meet the teacher's needs, for example, giving information about stress management, eating disorders, self-harm. This can then be part of an in-service training programme.

There are many training opportunities in Great Britain. Teachers or schools can contact the British Association for Counselling (BAC) (see the list of useful organizations and addresses on page 116) or local colleges and universities for information. It is important to ascertain the qualification awarded, and consider the relevance of the syllabus to the school environment.

Support

A teacher needs support not only in her teaching role but also in her pastoral work. Within the school there should be someone she can consult and with whom she can discuss ethical issues. Ideally this person should not be the person immediately above her in the line management. If consultation is used properly, a teacher will want to own feelings of helplessness, powerlessness, inadequacy – feelings that would be difficult to share with a line manager. Sadly, the more senior the teacher, often the less support there is available within the school. Where this is the case, support groups of senior teachers from several schools can be organized to share ideas about the work. For the newly qualified teacher there are different stresses. She may have fears about being seen as incompetent, and be apprehensive about sharing her concerns for fear of repercussions with references. Hence support again from someone who is not her line manager is recommended.

Egan (1986) refers to the difficulties of teaching during the first three years and asks whether mentors could ease the transition from student to novice to professional teacher. He suggests teaching can be a 'professional desert' for new staff, where communication is made difficult by the isolation of classroom experiences, by fear of discussing problems or asking too many questions, all of which carry the risk of appearing incompetent. It is for this reason that some schools use mentors to provide support and encouragement.

BAC stipulates that 'counselling supervision must be regular, consistent and appropriate to the counselling', and that 'non-managerial supervision is highly recommended' for those using counselling skills as part of their primary role (BAC 1998: B.6.3.3, 1999: D.3). The value of supervision is that it enhances the confidence, clarity and competence of the helper. It offers constructive ways of thinking about problems and above all is a safe, confidential place to discuss the work. It also offers help in recognizing and managing the emotional impact of such work.

Surveys on teacher stress and subsequent discussion on the subject have repeatedly shown that teachers suffer undue stress when they feel unsupported, undervalued or (worse still) criticized for the work they do. Supervision can be very cost-effective both in terms of managing students' problems and in preventing ill-health in teachers. Should ill-health result, BAC suggests a practitioner should 'withdraw from using counselling skills, temporarily or permanently, if their personal resources become sufficiently depleted to require this' (BAC 1999: D.4.3). However, where support, encouragement and supervision is available this is less necessary.

Summary

In this chapter I have looked at some of the issues a teacher needs to take into account when undertaking pastoral work. In the next chapter I consider how students may present their personal issues to a teacher and make practical suggestions as to how the teacher can respond.

Chapter 5

How students present issues

The concept of the presenting problem is frequently used in counselling and the counselling literature and merits an explanation. It refers to the initial presentation of a problem which may or may not be the only problem. It may be used to test the trustworthiness or helpfulness of the helper. This is not to say the 'presenting' problem is not important or real, but there may be other anxieties below the surface that are too difficult to raise and discuss in the first instance. For example, a student may present with problems about homework, choice of A levels and a Universities and Colleges Admissions Service (UCAS) application, whereas her underlying problem may be an eating disorder.

Trust is essential to helping. Some students find it difficult to trust, because they have not had good experiences of trustworthy adults and so are more likely to 'test' the trust. The ways students test trust include asking a favour; telling a small secret; asking questions; putting themselves down; inconveniencing the helper; forgetting an appointment; being late for appointments; and questioning the helper's motives.

It is easy to misconstrue a student's testing behaviours and react spontaneously rather than respond to the test of trust. Students find their own ways to test a teacher's trustworthiness, but some behaviours fall into recognizable patterns. Examples of 'testing' questions are, 'Are you a Catholic?', 'Have you ever tried cannabis?', or, 'Were you ever bullied at school?' At such times the teacher needs to respond to the underlying question. The response might then reflect the helper's ability to empathize with the student. So, the response to each of the above questions could be: 'Are you wondering if I can understand your dilemma if I'm not a Catholic, like you?', or, 'I guess you are wondering what my attitude to drugs is and wondering whether I can understand what is bothering you?', or, 'Do you wonder if I can really know what it is like to be bullied?'

Sometimes students send up a 'trial balloon' by telling the teacher a small secret. This might catch the listener off guard, and the teacher may find herself replying without having had a chance to think about the issue properly. Basically, a secret is asking the question, 'Are you safe enough for me to be vulnerable with you?' A common test is to tell the teacher a secret about a friend. If the teacher listens and accepts the confidence, and does not judge or criticize, the student may realize the teacher is trustworthy and non-judgmental.

Similarly, if a student asks a favour, it is how the request is handled that is important. It may be a test of willingness and reliability. Favours can be granted or denied according to their appropriateness, but the student will be able to discern the teacher's honesty from the reply. For example, if a student invites the teacher to a family christening, it is better to say, 'I'm sorry, I will have to say no to your invitation. I have a policy that I don't accept social invitations; but I will be interested to hear how it goes for you.' This is more honest than, 'Oh I'm sorry. I'll be away that weekend.' A student may pick up on non-verbal communication, perhaps a rise in speech rate or a hand gesture over the mouth, that communicates discomfort. The overall impression may be that the teacher is not being honest.

Some students arrive late or 'forget' appointments. In some circumstances there may be a practical reason for lateness, but it is also important to be aware of the possible testing nature of these behaviours. Some adolescents test the patience and tolerance of adults to the hilt, and some teachers may become exasperated by students who claim they want help but fail to avail themselves of it. By pushing adults to the limit these students sometimes appear to fulfil their own prediction that no one cares and so Lisa may say, 'I knew Mr Sims wasn't really bothered about me. When I got to his room, he'd already gone.' It is indeed frustrating, especially when time is so precious, to be tested in this way but it is helpful to recognize the behaviour as a test of trust.

Another way of testing the water is for students to put themselves down: 'I know this is really silly', 'You'll think I'm stupid', or even, 'You must think I'm mad.' Common opening lines are, 'You must see much worse problems than mine', or, 'I don't want to waste your time. I'm sure you've got much more serious problems to deal with than me.' The skill here is in addressing the underlying concern. Reassurance is inappropriate since it does not tackle the real worry. The teacher can say, 'Do you worry that I'll think you are silly?', or, 'Do you think I'll think your problem isn't very important?', or, 'Do you worry that I'll think you are wasting my time?' By addressing the concern in this way, a student can realize it is all right to be honest, and that it is safe to talk about worries.

Signs of underlying problems

Some students are able to identify clearly that they have a problem, and want time to talk about it. Other students may be less sure about asking for help and may not realize that help is available. Sometimes it becomes clear that a student is experiencing difficulties although the student has not yet identified for herself the need for help. One way that teachers can pick up on problems is by recognizing changes in a student. These might be in appearance, for example weight loss or condition of their skin or hair; or their work or attendance pattern; or their behaviour. Changes draw attention to the possibility of a problem.

Approaching students

The teacher is advised to proceed with caution since, while there may be a problem, the student may not wish to discuss it with the teacher and this wish has to be respected. A problem cannot be prised out of a student, but a comment to the effect that the teacher is willing to listen can be very helpful. She can say, 'I notice you've been seeming rather withdrawn lately. If you would like to talk about things, I'm sure we can find time to talk', or,

'I'm wondering if something is bothering you. If it is, just let me know, and I can arrange to see you.' It is helpful to keep the observation general and keep the offer to help open, rather than insist on talking to the student there and then. The student is then able to approach the teacher and say, 'You know you said I could come and talk to you . . .'. Other students may need to know that there are other people in school who may be able to help, for example, the school nurse.

Will help be resented?

Asking for help can involve all people, including adolescents, in some loss of self-esteem. It can be difficult to ask for help, so while a student may want help she may also resent it. Seeking help tends to reinforce in people their fears that they are inadequate. The skill of the helper is to help the student to find her own solutions rather than impose solutions on her, so helping a student in fact is an empowering process not a disabling one, but a student may not realize this initially. If a student can be helped to acquire a greater understanding into herself and her problems, the process will increase her self-esteem and confidence in herself. The teacher, in this helping capacity, does not have answers, even though she may have her own ideas about a solution. It is important for a student to feel safe enough to explore her conflicts, her problems and for her to arrive at her own understanding. At times there may not be a 'solution' as such, but rather a coming to terms with the reality of events, for example losses through death, divorce, separation or disability.

Not all students want help within school. It may be obvious to the teacher that a student is under considerable stress but the student cannot be made to accept help. At such times it may be better to refer to someone outside school (see making a referral later in this chapter). The reasons for this may be to do with trust, confidentiality, or a concern about lack of understanding, especially if the student is in a minority group because of her gender, class, race, religion, sexual orientation or disability. Appropriate information can then be given to the student about national and local resources (see the list of useful organizations and addresses on page 116).

The counselling relationship has to be freely entered into and cannot be the subject of conditions. For instance, if a student faces suspension for bullying she cannot be offered counselling as a condition or as an alternative to punishment. If the student wishes to explore her bullying behaviour this has to be her decision made separately from any disciplinary procedures.

Resistance

Most people seeking help present some degree of resistance. Although they want help, part of them does not want to change, and this is normal because change can be painful. Counselling is not a comfortable process, especially since it involves self-examination and most people find this hard to do without becoming self-critical. It is not easy to change behaviour or to examine painful feelings. Understanding the nature of resistance to change is fundamental to the helping process and unless it is recognized, the helper is likely to feel frustrated and thwarted in her efforts. It may be displayed in a variety of ways:

- silence
- hostility
- over-compliance
- denial of the need for help, especially with an eating disorder, alcohol or drug abuse, self-harm
- excessive talkativeness or small talk
- retreat into humour

It is important when a teacher recognizes signs of resistance not to feel she is failing. She may feel irritated, rejected, resentful, or confused. Resistance is not the helper's 'fault' but rather a demonstration of a student's natural apprehension or ambivalence about being helped. Unless a teacher understands this and accepts her own feelings she may find herself being impatient, feeling half-hearted, blaming; she may try to coax the student; she may lower her expectations of herself and of the student, or even give up on the helping.

Silence

Sometimes in a student silence is the result of a lack of skills in the helper; sometimes it is about the student's anxiety about the purpose and possible consequences of a meeting. It can also indicate that there is not yet enough trust established for the student to speak. At such times the helper's ability to empathize comes to the rescue. She can reflect on the student's difficulty in talking. She can avoid asking a lot of questions, particularly closed questions. The teacher can say, 'Perhaps you feel anxious about coming to see me. You may be wondering how confidential our discussion can be?', 'Perhaps you feel a bit uncertain about the purpose of this meeting?', or, 'It can be difficult to know where to begin.'

Hostility

Some students may be sceptical of the helping process. Others may be hostile to offers of help particularly if they feel they are being pushed into counselling; have no choice in the matter; or have been labelled as 'mad' or 'bad'. Clarification of the purpose of the meeting and how counselling works is helpful. Voluntary participation is basic to effective counselling.

Over-compliance

Certain students may feel they have to be polite and have to please adults. Their experiences may lead them to fear rejection or criticism if they are not compliant. Such students may find it difficult to express how they really feel.

Denial of the need for help

Students may be reluctant to give up their symptoms especially if their symptoms 'work' for them. For example, an eating disorder can be seen as a way of dealing with problems but the student may not be ready or willing to address the underlying issues.

Students who talk excessively

Some students mask their anxiety by talkativeness. There may be difficult feelings below the surface but the small talk keeps them at bay. The teacher can help by staying calm and not engaging in the small talk. She can acknowledge the initial difficulty in coming for help and gently pull the student back to the purpose of the meeting and focus on the important issues.

Retreat into humour

This may indicate that a student is anxious and finds talking about personal matters difficult. Humour can serve as a means of avoiding painful issues.

Student presentations

It can be misleading to generalize but some general points can be made about certain presentations. Here I include some ideas about students who appear to be reluctant, angry, who 'act out' or who can be identified as being more 'vulnerable', and hence more likely to need the counselling skills of the teacher.

Reluctant students

Voluntary participation in any counselling activity is basic to effective helping. Students may be reluctant to accept help or ask for help for a variety of reasons. For instance the student may:

- be unclear about the purpose of the meeting
- be unclear about the ramifications of any meeting (for example, parents being informed)
- have had bad experiences in the past and be suspicious of helpers
- construe needing help as being a sign of weakness or of failure
- not understand the process of 'counselling'
- need to test the helper's level of support and commitment

- not see any need to change her behaviour or reflect on her circumstances
- feel coerced or pressurized to accept help
- not like the helper

Other variables such as gender, prejudice, race, religion, social class and cultural norms can also play a part. For instance, some black students may find it difficult to believe a white teacher can be understanding. The following guidelines can be used to deal more effectively with reluctant students.

- Explore the purpose of the meeting, the limits of confidentiality and the time available.
- Acknowledge and help the student deal with feelings of reluctance. (For example, 'You probably have mixed feelings about coming here?', or, 'I guess you feel angry about being sent to see me.')
- Provide an accepting, warm and empathic atmosphere, that is, create a safe environment in which difficult or 'negative' feelings can be expressed.
- Explain the helping process and the teacher's role within it.
- Allow space for the student to talk about her feelings and explore their root causes.
- Avoid confrontation and interpretation.
- Respond to the feelings expressed.
- Allow the student freedom to stay or leave while making it clear the purpose of the meeting is to listen and help rather than judge and discipline.
- Suggest other people both in and outside school who may be able to help if this offer of help is rejected.

Angry students

The nature of anger and aggression is still much debated and particularly how much it is innate and how much it is a response to frustration or fear. Beneath many displays of anger there is often sadness, helplessness and emptiness. Anger is a natural feeling but problems can arise as a result of the way people express it. Sometimes people turn their anger outwards and attack others physically or verbally. Others direct it towards themselves and the result can be depression, self-harm, an eating disorder, drug or alcohol abuse. Mature relating should be able to include the verbal expression of anger rather than acting out destructive feelings.

Some people respond to hurt and injustice by being angry. In this sense anger is defensive and protects the person from further hurt. What can be very helpful with students who are angry is to identify the feeling; accept it; look at the cause of it; try to understand it and finally decide on appropriate action. Sometimes this is easier to do after the event, for obvious reasons, but by looking back on an incident this kind of analysis can take place and alternative actions be explored. This offers new strategies that can be employed the next time the student is in the heat of an angry outburst. Being offered appropriate ways to discharge feelings can be empowering. For instance, if Sonia gets angry in a lesson she may need to learn it is better to leave the classroom and take time out, rather than hit out in explosive rage. Her feelings need to be addressed, but more appropriate ways can be found to deal with her anger and frustration. Similarly if Tara's sister is being bullied, Tara is entitled to feel angry, but if she attacks the bully herself, her behaviour is not acceptable.

Some people grow up believing it is 'wrong' to have certain feelings and feel ashamed of having or expressing 'bad' feelings such as anger, jealousy or envy. What can be acknowledged is that such feelings are legitimate. They are neither good nor bad in themselves. What is at issue is how such feelings are expressed.

Acting out students

Acting out is a specific term describing a person who acts damagingly outside the counselling session instead of verbally expressing her thoughts and feelings in the session. In school, the term can be applied to behaviour which indirectly communicates a student's distress. For example, a student may engage in substance abuse or inappropriate sexual relationships; may steal or self-harm. This kind of behaviour is a communication even if it is difficult to tolerate or understand. Because a student's distress is 'acted out', it is much harder to understand than when a problem is talked about. The student who 'acts out' is likely to need help, but is all the more difficult to assist because her distress cannot be verbalized. Such students may need help to put it into words or may need to be referred to specialist agencies.

Vulnerable students

It goes without saying that the adolescents who are most at risk are not necessarily the ones who most obviously show it. However, certain students may be said to be more vulnerable than others, including those who:

- have recently experienced the death of a close family member or friend
- have lost a parent or sibling in their childhood
- have a family history of mental or physical illness
- have a history of family violence
- come from a family of high achievers, where there may be pressure to achieve equally highly
- are from minority groups in respect of race, religion, disability, gender, sexual orientation
- are withdrawn and isolated
- express bizarre behaviour or ideas

The teacher needs to be alert to the possibility of problems, which may be less obvious than with the disruptive student.

Dealing with suicidal threats, crises and disclosures

Suicidal threats

Adolescents are particularly prone to depression and mood swings and thoughts of suicide are common, even if very disturbing for parents, teachers and peers. Adolescence is a transitional period and as such brings developmental crises. When suicidal thoughts or threats are expressed they should always be taken seriously.

Whether it is by inference or by explicit statement, the subject should always be brought into the open. It is essential to advise the student to see her GP. It is one of the few occasions when advice can be given and when confidentiality cannot be guaranteed, both for the student's and the teacher's sake. On rare occasions, if the student refuses to see her GP, the teacher will have to tell the student that she needs to contact the GP herself. In such cases it is vital to tell the student of this intention, rather than for her to find out later. If the teacher does not inform the student this is likely to be seen as a betrayal of trust. She may not like the teacher for contacting the GP, but eventually she will register the teacher's concern and the fact that she is being taken seriously.

When the subject is brought into the open, it is then possible to see if there is any evidence of planning. It is more serious and worrying if there is a threat involving a planned trip to a lonely spot; or letters being written to family and friends; or tablets being bought or saved up. Such threats merit a calm but immediate response. Most students who mention suicide take no action. However, the risk can never be underestimated. Occasionally a student does commit suicide without hinting to anyone that there was a serious problem. The precipitating event may have been a relationship breakdown, failed exams or the result of alcohol or drug abuse. Following such a tragedy the deceased family, friends and teachers are likely to feel very distressed, guilty and even angry. Such feelings are normal and need to be expressed. Formal counselling may be indicated.

Crises

Crises are stressful experiences that are usually sudden or unexpected and demand a lot of the sufferer's energy and attention. They may be due to loss, for example a death or parents separating; or to transitions, for example moving house or changing school; or to unexpected events, for example an accident or hospitalization. At such times students may find the support from family and friends insufficient. Feelings threaten to overwhelm them. One of the most important responses is to stay calm, even though the subject matter is very distressing. The aim is to contain the student's feelings. The teacher may find that she needs additional support, so that her own feelings do not spill over to the student. The following guidelines will assist in such situations:

- Remain calm and stable. The student's feelings are likely to be strong and powerful. It is important that the teacher controls her own anxieties and emotions.
- The student is likely to feel calmer simply as a result of sharing her feelings. If the teacher uses empathic responses she will help the student feel understood.
- Allow the student to speak and not interrupt, least of all to share the teacher's own feelings.
- Deal with the immediate situation rather than look for underlying causes. These can be addressed after the crisis has passed.
- Ascertain the amount of support available to the student.
- Be aware of local resources.
- Assess the risk to the student and mobilize additional support if necessary, for example school nurse, school counsellor, social worker.
- Help the student decide what needs to be done, and help her prioritize.
- Make use of the teacher's own personal support system.

The main behaviours to avoid are trying to cheer up the student, expressing platitudes and trying to solve the problem for her. The essence of dealing with a crisis is to stay calm, let the person vent their feelings and deal with the immediate situation. For example, if Hayley tells you she had unprotected sex last night, the issues around contraception can wait. The priority is to seek medical advice which may involve determining whether or not the morning-after pill is required.

Disclosures

Sometimes children disclose or make allegations of abuse to teachers. In such circumstances teachers need to proceed with particular caution. They need to be aware that the way they talk to a child can have an effect on evidence put forward in any subsequent criminal proceedings. Teachers should not ask a child leading questions, since this can be interpreted as putting ideas into a child's mind. It is preferable to say, 'Tell me what happened' than ask, 'Did they do (this) to you?'

The main aim when dealing with a potential disclosure is to listen to the child without interrupting if he or she is freely recalling significant events. Notes should be made as soon as possible after the conversation has taken place and the information passed to the designated teacher. The note should record the time, date, place and people who were present, as well as what was said. The teacher's notes may be used in subsequent court hearings. If a teacher or another member of staff is accused of abuse, procedures should be followed in accordance with local Area Child Protection Committee (ACPC) practice. Children who report abuse must be listened to and heard. No suggestions must be made to the child or alternative explanations offered. A written, dated record of the allegation should be made as soon as possible, preferably within 24 hours.

Teachers cannot promise total confidentiality to students who make such allegations. The teacher should listen to the allegation and seek to involve the child in any decision to take the allegation further. When a child says she does not wish to take the matter further, very careful consideration should be given to the age and understanding of the child, and whether the child or others may be at risk of significant harm. Teachers need to inform students that in some circumstances they are bound to pass on this type of information.

According to DfEE Circular 10/95 (1995b) it is acknowledged that children with special education needs (SEN) may be especially vulnerable to abuse (paragraph 36). The circular advises: 'Where abuse is suspected, pupils who have difficulties in communicating should be given the chance to express themselves to a member of staff with appropriate communication skills. Designated teachers should work with SEN coordinators to identify pupils with SEN and their communication needs' (paragraph 37) (see Chapter 6).

Making a referral

When it comes to making a referral it is important for a teacher to be familiar with the range of services available in the community offered by the National Health Service and voluntary organizations. It is helpful to have national directories in school as well as details of local resources. Year heads often have a wealth of knowledge that they have accumulated but it is very useful for all staff to have access to actual lists of resources. National organizations relating to a specific problem are listed on page 116 and further details can be obtained from libraries, Citizens Advice Bureaux or telephone directories.

There is a policy in all schools as to who should write letters of referral and who should make contact with outside agencies. It is important that there is a structure or a filtering system so that if a form tutor is concerned about a student, these concerns can be shared with the year head (with the student's permission), and an appropriate course of action can be taken. It is likely that a senior teacher will already be involved if the problem is serious, but good liaison is essential, so that both the student and the tutor are involved in the process.

There may be several reasons for making a referral to an outside agency. The most common relate to the teacher's level of competence, and to the limits of her responsibilities. Sometimes personal factors play a part, for example, the teacher holds strong conflicting values or too closely identifies with the problem. A teacher needs to recognize when specialist help is required, for example, depression; self-harm; eating disorders; panic attacks; phobias; alcohol and drug misuse. This is not a measure of her ability but is a matter of professional judgement. Once the need for specialist help has been identified the teacher needs to use her skills to encourage the student to accept help; she needs to make the referral and to provide ongoing support until the new helping relationship is established.

When making the suggestion that specialist help is indicated, tact is required so that the student does not feel rejected. The teacher must be honest, and say that a problem is beyond her expertise. She may say, 'I don't know enough about this problem to be able to help you, but I know there are people who could help you', or, 'I do want to help you, but I don't think I know enough about this subject. I wonder if it would be better for us to think about contacting someone who is able to help?' A teacher can reassure that her support will still be available and that she is interested in what happens, even if she is not going to be able to help directly.

If a referral has to be made to another agency, the cooperation of a student is important. Sometimes it is a matter of careful
timing. Much time can be wasted with failed appointments if
the student does not agree to the referral. The student may have
mixed feelings about the referral, which an agency will have to
address, but in the main it is desirable that the student agrees
to the referral. Sometimes giving a student a few days to think
about the suggestion can make a considerable difference. The
student then feels she has a free choice and is not being pushed
into a course of action. Gentle encouragement is likely to be more
effective than insistence. Admitting that there is a problem is a
major step, but further time may be needed to acknowledge that
professional help is required. This is particularly evident with
an eating disorder when the problem is frequently denied. The
teacher can say, 'From what you have been telling me, Anne-
Marie, I'm wondering if it would be a good idea to get in touch
with your GP. What do you think?' Anne-Marie may reply, 'No,
there's no point really. I'm okay', to which the teacher can say,
'Well, I can tell you're not keen on the idea. What I'd like you to
do is to think about it. Then, when I see you next week, perhaps
we can talk about it again. How would that be?'

Some students have fears and fantasies about the psychi-
atric services. They fear being labelled as 'mad' or as a 'mental
case'. They may be apprehensive about the reactions of their
friends or their family. They may also be anxious that details
will be put on to UCAS or job application forms. It is worth
exploring a student's fears about any referral. Fears need to be
listened to, not dismissed as 'silly' or 'irrational'. The teacher can
say, 'I can see you are a bit apprehensive about going to see a
psychiatrist. I wonder what you think they do?' The student
may reply, 'Well, they only see mad people and give them drugs so
that they don't know what they are doing.' Here a little information can put a student's mind at rest. The teacher can explain,
'Child and adolescent psychiatrists are doctors who specialize
in working with young people who have emotional problems.
Usually they like to meet the family and just talk about the
problem. They can prescribe drugs if necessary but they do listen
to what parents and the person concerned says about taking
medication.' The student may respond, 'But don't they expect
you to lie on a couch and say everything that comes into your

mind?' The teacher can clarify, 'That sounds like a psychoanalyst who is different from a psychiatrist. Child psychiatrists work with children and young people all the time. They sit and talk to them just like you and me now.' Accurate knowledge is important.

Reassurance ('You'll be okay', or, 'There's nothing to worry about') does not work. It is necessary to explore worries and see if any fears can be dispelled. It is not advisable to mention personal experiences of psychiatrists or being prescribed anti-depressants. Inappropriate information only burdens a student whose circumstances may be quite different (see self-disclosure in Chapter 4).

At times it may be necessary to meet a student's parents and discuss the need for a referral. Such meetings again need to be handled sensitively. Parents will take time to accept the fact that their child needs help. They will easily feel judged, criticized or blamed. Some time taken exploring their worries in the early stages can save much time later on. With regard to the student it is important to be clear about the purpose of any meeting with her parents. She needs to know what will be discussed and what the teacher is likely to say. She needs to be clear about what is confidential and what will be shared with her parents. If the student is not invited to join the meeting, feedback should be given to her. If she is to benefit from any help, she has to feel involved and not be the passive recipient of help. Unless her cooperation is gained she is likely to fail to keep appointments. As a general rule parents need to be involved in their child's welfare although there will be times when students do not want this. Students may decide to go it alone in seeking contraceptive advice, counselling or in getting in touch with national organiza-tions such as the Eating Disorders Association or a self-help group. This is their decision, but it can present ethical dilemmas for the teacher since it raises questions about professional judgement and confidentiality (see confidentiality in Chapter 6).

If a referral is made to an outside agency, information should be restricted to as few people as possible. Liaison with form tutors and perhaps subject teachers is necessary but details can be kept to a minimum. It is advisable for the student to be asked for permission to tell her tutor, or at the very least she should be told who has been given information and what they have been told. In regard to a referral letter it is helpful to discuss its contents with a student, since this will help her feel involved and maintain trust. The following guidelines about making a referral may also be of value:

- Be familiar with the school's policy for making referrals. On what basis should a referral be made? By whom? Whom to consult? Who has ongoing responsibility? What information is to be recorded and where? What are the parent's rights?
- Obtain information on the community resources and what sort of help they offer.
- Explore the student's readiness for referral.
- Be honest and explain that additional help is needed. Care is needed so that the student does not feel rejected.
- Ascertain the waiting list of the agency.
- Liaise with the parents whenever possible.
- Explain the services of the agency so that expectations are realistic.
- Allow the student time to get used to the idea and involve her in the process.
- Do not release information about the student without her consent.
- Offer ongoing support.

Summary

Working with young people raises many issues and questions for professionals who come into contact with them and teachers are no exception. One of the major concerns relates to the legal position of teachers in respect of confidentiality, child protection, sex education and drug misuse. It is these issues that are the subject of the next chapter.

Chapter 6

Teachers' legal liabilities and responsibilities

It is not surprising that many teachers report confusion about their legal liabilities and responsibilities, especially in relation to pastoral work and to issues of confidentiality. The law of education is contained in many Acts of Parliament from which flow statutory instruments, circulars and administrative memoranda. For example, the Education Act 1993 requires certain schools to provide sex education (Section 241 (2)). But besides the requirements as laid down in the Act there are also DfEE circulars which are sent to schools. These are not legally binding. They do not represent an authoritative statement of the law since only the courts can provide that. For example, DfEE Circular 5/94 (DfEE 1994a) explains the changes made by the Education Act 1993 in the law governing the provision of sex education in maintained schools in England and Wales and offers guidance to local education authorities (LEAs) and schools on implementation. The law here refers to maintained county, voluntary, maintained special and grant maintained schools in England and Wales. It should be noted that the Education Act 1993 has been repealed and replaced by the Education Act 1996, but the new Act still requires maintained secondary schools to provide sex education.

In Box 6.1 I list the teacher's legal liabilities and responsibilities as laid down in DfEE Circular 4/98 (DfEE 1998).

While all these matters are essential for any teacher to under-

Box 6.1: Teachers' legal liabilities and responsibilities

DfEE 4/98 states that 'those to be awarded Qualified Teacher Status should, when assessed, demonstrate that they have a working knowledge and understanding of':

- the Race Relations Act 1976
- the Sex Discrimination Act 1975
- Sections 7 and 8 of the Health and Safety at Work etc. Act 1974
- common law duty to ensure that pupils are healthy and safe on school premises and when leading activities off the school site, such as educational visits, school outings or field trips
- what is reasonable for the purposes of safeguarding or promoting Children's Welfare (Section 3 (5) of the Children Act 1989)
- the role of the educational service in protecting children from abuse (currently set out in DfEE Circular 10/95 (DfEE 1995b) and the Home Office, Department of Health, DfEE and Welsh Office Guidance, *Working Together Under the Children Act 1989: A Guide to Arrangements for Inter-agency Co-operation for the Protection of Children from abuse*; Home Office 1991)
- appropriate physical contact with pupils (currently set out in DfEE Circular 10/95; DfEE 1995b)
- appropriate physical restraint of pupils (Section 4 of the Education Act 1997 and DfEE Circular 9/94; DfEE 1994b)
- detention of pupils on disciplinary grounds (Section 5 of the Education Act 1997)

stand, of specific relevance for the teacher who is engaged in any pastoral work are the laws and guidance circulars related to the protection of children from abuse. The relevant texts are:

- the Children Act 1989
- *Working Together Under the Children Act 1989* (Home Office 1991)
- DfEE Circular 10/95 (DfEE 1995b)

The Children Act 1989

The purpose of the Children Act 1989 is to simplify child welfare law by repealing a vast body of legislation and replacing it with a single statutory framework which reflects a coherent set of legal concepts and principles. The main principles embodied in this Act are that parents share responsibility for their children and should be left to do so until things go wrong or they need help. If help is then provided it should be on the basis of what is best for the child.

The role of public authorities is seen as one that should help rather than undermine the parents. However, it is concluded that public authorities may have to take over if the children are going to suffer harm. The Act intends that authorities should act in partnership with the family. It also recognizes that children have a right to a voice in decisions about their lives and a developing right to take some of those decisions for themselves.

Section 3 (5) allows a teacher to do what is reasonable in all the circumstances of the case for the purpose of safeguarding or promoting the child's welfare, that is, to act as a reasonable parent would do.

Section 47 is concerned with child protection. It states that the police and social services department have a duty to investigate when they 'have reasonable cause to believe that a child living or found in their area is suffering or likely to suffer significant harm'. The wording emphasizes a current concern rather than a past cause of concern and is clear that there is or will be real risk of harm occurring.

Protecting children from abuse

While social services have a duty to investigate, teachers are bound by local authority rules to liaise with social services. The Children Act 1989 is specific in requiring relevant information to be contributed by anyone working with a young person during an enquiry. Inter-agency cooperation is recommended and is made explicit in the document *Working Together Under the Children Act 1989* (Home Office 1991: 27). It states: 'any person who has knowledge of, or a suspicion that a child is suffering significant harm should refer their concern to one or more of the agencies with statutory duties and/or powers to investigate and intervene – the social services department, the police or the National Society for the Prevention of Cruelty to Children (NSPCC)'. Where there is a risk to the life of the child or a likelihood of serious injury, the first priority must be to secure the immediate safety of the child. Children have a right to protection; hence allegations and suspicions of abuse have to be taken seriously and appropriate procedures followed according to local Area Child Protection Committee (ACPC) policy. The Children Act 1989 (Section 47) states that there is a duty upon those workers employed by local authorities, including education and health services, to assist social services in their enquiries in the case of child abuse where called upon to do so but not where doing so would be unreasonable in all the circumstances of the case. However, some area child protection procedures do not allow the 'unreasonable circumstance' clause and insist that all allegations of abuse are reported immediately to the designated teacher.

All staff need to be alert to signs of abuse, to be aware of ACPC procedures and to inform the designated member of staff of any concerns. *Working Together Under the Children Act 1989* (Home Office 1991: 21) states: 'Teachers and other school staff are particularly well placed to observe outward signs of abuse, changes in behaviour or failure to develop.' Circular 10/95 (DfEE 1995b) clarifies this point and suggests that possible indicators of physical neglect, emotional or sexual abuse may be noticeable but can only be taken as signs which give rise to concern and suspicion. Any concerns should be discussed with the designated teacher who has specific responsibility for child protection. It is not the responsibility of teachers to investigate any suspected abuse. The procedures for dealing with cases of suspected abuse are clearly laid out by the local ACPC. With regard to children with special education needs (SEN), who may be regarded as especially vulnerable to abuse the position is clarified. Paragraph 36 of the circular states, 'Extra care should be taken to interpret correctly apparent signs of abuse and neglect. Indications of abuse of these children should be reported exactly as for other children according to locally established procedures' (DfEE 1995b).

Guidance concerning interviews in cases of suspected sexual abuse comes in the Butler-Sloss Report (DHSS 1988). The report states clearly that interviewing is an extremely skilled and difficult task for which the interviewer must have training, experience and aptitude. It is recognized that inappropriate and unskilled work can be very damaging to the young person.

The Children Act 1989 does not clarify the rights of children with regard to confidentiality and counselling. This means that ethical dilemmas can and do arise for professionals who are working with children as they seek to reconcile the legal requirement to share information about a young person's allegations of abuse with a young person's request for confidentiality. This was recognized in the Butler-Sloss Report (DHSS 1988) which recommends: 'Professionals should not make promises which cannot be kept to a child and in the light of possible court proceedings should not promise a child that what was told in confidence can be kept in confidence.'

Child protection raises issues of confidentiality which need to be understood by all teachers. Paragraph 27 of Circular 10/95 states:

Staff have a professional responsibility to share relevant information about the protection of children with other professionals, particularly investigative agencies. If a child confides in a member of staff and requests that the information is kept secret, it is important that the member of staff tells the child sensitively that he or she has a responsibility to refer cases of alleged abuse to the appropriate agencies for the child's own sake. Within that context, the child should, however, be assured that the matter will be disclosed only to people who need to know about it.

(DfEE 1995b)

Working Together Under the Children Act 1989 (Home Office 1991: 13) emphasizes the need for confidentiality: 'In child protection work the degree of confidentiality will be governed by the need to protect the child . . . Confidentiality may not be maintained if the withholding of the information will prejudice the welfare of a child.'

Confidentiality

Confidentiality is basic to counselling, because by its very nature counselling involves a close relationship in which a person reveals intimate details about their life. This can only happen where trust and confidentiality can be offered. Courts expect counsellors to maintain high standards of practice about confidentiality, but do not recognize any absolute privilege about not disclosing information. Only barristers and solicitors have this absolute privilege. In practice, there are only a few circumstances in which counsellors may be obliged to break confidentiality. The major exception relates to the Prevention of Terrorism (Temporary Provisions) Act 1989, Chapter 4.

A teacher is in a very different position from a counsellor and cannot promise confidentiality. If she adopts the BAC *Code of Ethics and Practice Guidelines for Those Using Counselling Skills in their Work* it is clear that high standards of confidentiality are expected, but in school her primary role is that of a teacher. She has to abide by LEA and school policies. She can listen to students and exercise her professional judgement as to whether or not to share information, but she cannot promise confidentiality. There is no legislation that deals specifically with confidentiality in schools. Teachers cannot promise total confidentiality and a student has no legal right to expect confidentiality. Teachers should consult school policy with respect to confidentiality regarding sex education or drugs.

School policies

The DfEE publication, *School Governors: A Guide to the Law* (1997: 133) states that the governing body of a school is required by law to provide policy statements and publications. See Box 6.2.

Schools may draw up policies on other issues such as bullying, drug misuse, dress code and confidentiality. A policy regarding confidentiality could be useful to explain the situations in which teachers may have to disclose information that is told to them in confidence. Parents, students and staff should be made aware of the school's policy and of the limits to confidentiality. In individual cases, teachers should act within the school's agreed

---

Box 6.2: Policies and publications required by law

- *Action Plan* following school inspection
- *Admissions Policy* (if LEA transfers the responsibility to them)
- *Annual Governors' Report to Parents*
- *Charging Policy*
- *Curriculum Aims*
- *Curriculum Complaints Procedure* (grant maintained (GM) schools only)
- *Health and Safety Policy* (aided and GM schools only)
- *Prospectus*
- *Pupil Discipline*
- *Staff Discipline*
- *Standing Orders* (GM schools only)
- *Special Educational Needs Policy*
- *Sex Education* (all secondary schools)

---

policy. If a teacher believes that a student may be about to reveal information which the teacher will have to disclose, the student needs to be told about this. When it is in the best interests of a young person to pass on any of the information that is disclosed, confidentiality must be maintained between those professionals who need to be informed. A student can at least be reassured that this will be the case.

Passing on information

Many professionals interpret the moral duty to pass on information narrowly. The two situations in which most professionals feel a breach of confidence is justified is where there is a child protection issue or where the life of the young person or third party is at risk. If a decision is made that it is in the child's best interests to pass on information to other agencies, the teacher should seek to obtain the child's prior consent. The child should also be informed of the likely outcome of the information being passed on to another agency.

There is no legal duty for teachers to inform parents if a student discloses something to them. It is a matter of professional judgement as to whether or not such information should be kept confidential. It may be seen as good practice to communicate with parents about the young person's need and this should be with the student's permission. The overriding principle in all cases is the welfare of the child and the best interests of the child. This may involve encouraging a young person to talk to their parents or guardians and offering support to do this. It may involve keeping confidences.

A teacher does not have a general duty to inform the head teacher of disclosures made by a student. The decision as to whether or not to do so must be a matter of the teacher's discretion. However, if a teacher is called upon by the head teacher to reveal the disclosure, the teacher is professionally bound to do so and failure to do so could be grounds for disciplinary action. When the decision involves allegations of child abuse, the information must be passed to the person designated under child protection procedures. As I have stressed, students must be clear about whether their confidentiality will be respected. Ideally, the position should be explained to them before any disclosures are made. They need to know that the school and its teachers aim to respect their confidences, but that there are times when teachers have to act, such as when there is a concern about the student's protection and safety. They should be made aware of:

- the limits of confidentiality
- the system of support within the school
- the system of referral to other agencies not the school
- other agencies available to help them
- what information is recorded on the school's records, and whether or not they can have access to them.

Other relevant information

Besides being familiar with child protection procedures, a teacher needs to be familiar with the law and guidance in respect of:

- sex education
- medical treatment

- drugs
- criminal activity
- access to records
- physical contact.

Sex education

Since 1994 all maintained, county, voluntary, maintained special and grant maintained secondary schools in England and Wales have been required by law to provide sex education, including information on HIV and Aids and other sexually transmitted diseases, to all registered pupils (Education Act 1996, chapter 56). Sex education is not compulsory in Scottish schools nor is there specific guidance issued by the Scottish Office. Teachers working in Scotland should consult the regional guidelines on sex education.

Young people in England and Wales have a right to sex education contained within the National Curriculum. However, parents have an absolute right to withdraw their child from sex education classes outside the National Curriculum. The only exception to this parental right is when the young person wants to attend the lessons, and the young person (or someone acting on their behalf) applies to the court for a 'specific issue order' under Section 8 of the Children Act 1989. This is only likely to happen in exceptional circumstances.

Teachers in independent schools are not covered by the National Curriculum, the law relating to sex education or the Department for Education Circular 5/94 (DfEE 1994a). These teachers are advised to find out whether their school policy permits them to offer information on contraceptive services, and whether such information can be kept confidential.

The government requires that LEAs, governing bodies and head teachers take steps to ensure that sex education encourages pupils to have 'regard to moral considerations and the value of family life' (Education Act (No. 2) 1986: paragraph 4). Guidance as to how sex education should be considered is found in DfEE Circular 5/94 (DfEE 1994a). As Beloff and Mountfield (1994) state: 'it is advisory only and has no special legal status. Teachers are not obliged to follow its advice. However, if a head teacher requires staff to follow the advice, they should do so.'

The circular offers the following guidance concerning advice to individual pupils: 'There will be occasions when teachers have to exercise their discretion and judgement about how to deal with particularly explicit issues raised by an individual pupil. It is unlikely to be appropriate to deal with such issues with the whole class. Teachers should normally discuss such concerns with the child's parents first to see how they would like the matter to be handled. It may be appropriate for the teacher to speak individually to the child before consulting the parents, to clarify the basis for the concerns. Where there is a risk that a teacher might be compromised in these circumstances, it would be wise for them to be accompanied by another member of staff' (paragraph 31).

Paragraphs 38–40 explain: 'It is important to distinguish between, on the one hand, the school's function of providing education generally about sexual matters and on the other, counselling and advice to individual pupils on these issues, particularly if this relates to their own sexual behaviour. Good teachers have always taken a pastoral interest in the welfare and well-being of pupils. But this function should never trespass on the proper exercise of parental rights and responsibilities. Particular care must be exercised in relation to contraceptive advice to pupils under 16 for whom sexual intercourse is unlawful. The general rule must be that giving an individual pupil advice on such matters without parental knowledge or consent would be an inappropriate exercise of a teacher's professional responsibilities. Teachers are not health professionals and the legal position of a teacher giving advice in such circumstances has never been tested in the courts. The teacher should encourage the pupil to seek advice from his or her parents and if appropriate from the relevant health service professional. Teachers should inform the head teacher if a pupil has embarked upon or is contemplating a course of conduct which is likely to place him or her at moral or physical risk or is in breach of the law' (paragraph 40). The Brook Advisory Centres (1996: 11) give clear guidance to teachers regarding information and advice on contraception to pupils under 16:

Teachers are not health professionals, so should not give an individual young person advice on which method of contraception to use. A teacher should encourage a student to seek parental advice and may encourage a student to refer to appropriate health professionals or to a clinic for advice on individual circumstances. The guiding principle for a teacher should be to act in the best interests of the young person he or she has spoken to. A teacher's role is in the educational context. Providing general information about contraception is part of a school's sex education programme and is distinct from giving advice to individual pupils on questions which are the province of health professionals. Where teachers are following their schools' policy on sex education and are within the guidelines described here, they can be confident of acting within the law by providing information about contraception.

In practice this means that teachers in secondary schools can discuss general issues relating to contraception if they arise as part of the teaching of any subject. They can also provide information on local contraceptive services unless the school's sex education policy states otherwise. This applies to those under and over the age of 16. Teachers can give under-16s information about an appropriate health professional or clinic to visit and explain that the consultation with the health professional will be confidential. They can give this information even if the parents have withdrawn the young person from sex education classes outside the National Curriculum, unless the school sex education policy states otherwise.

If a student under 16 asks a teacher to make an appointment on his or her behalf, the teacher can inform the young person of an appropriate health professional or clinic that might be contacted. The teacher needs to check the school policy to see if she can make an appointment for a student under 16, or if she can accompany the student to an appointment. Teachers should not give an individual young person advice on which method of contraception to use. A teacher should encourage a student to seek parental advice, and may encourage a student to refer to appropriate health professionals or to a clinic. The guiding principle for a teacher should be to act in the best interests of the young person, which involves using her professional judgement.

Homosexuality

Many teachers are confused about the legal situation regarding teaching about homosexuality in the classroom and in particular about the relevance of Section 28 of the Local Government Act 1988. DfEE Circular 5/94 states:

> Section 2 of the Local Government Act 1986 (as amended by Section 28 of the Local Government Act 1988) prohibits local authorities from intentionally promoting homo-sexuality or publishing material with that intention, and from promoting the teaching in any maintained school of the acceptability of homosexuality as a pretended family relationship. This prohibition applies to the activities of local authorities themselves, as distinct from the activities of the governing bodies and staff of schools on their own behalf.
>
> (DfEE 1994a)

Section 28 does not apply to schools and should not affect the delivery of sex education in the classroom. There is no prohibition in law for schools and teachers to look at issues of sexuality.

The Gillick ruling

The Gillick decision in the House of Lords about the rights of children under 16 years old represents a landmark towards giving children and young people greater rights with regard to confidentiality. A young person who has sufficient understanding and intelligence to give a legally valid consent to medical treatment is now often referred to as a 'Gillick competent child'. Deciding whether or not a young person is of sufficient understanding and intelligence is a matter of assessment. This assessment is very important, because it forms the basis for deciding whether or not parents ought to be consulted. On this point the Children's Legal Centre (1996: 3) states: 'While there is no legal decision which sets a minimum age at which children can be regarded as competent to consent to their own medical treatment, it is unlikely that many children under the age of 13 would be deemed competent to consent to medical treatment or counselling without the involvement of the parent.'

In practice this means that parents do not need to be consulted before contraceptive advice or treatment is given, as long as the young person has sufficient understanding and intelligence. Similarly young people requiring counselling, who have sufficient understanding and intelligence, do not have to consult their parents, nor does the counsellor have to inform the parents that counselling is or has been taking place. The Children Act 1989 also accepts the principle of the 'Gillick competent child', but does not further clarify the rights of children with regard to confidentiality and counselling.

The term 'Gillick competent' does not mean that a child can refuse treatment. The law does not allow young people to refuse life-saving treatment. In the case of a young person threatening suicide or similar action, there is a general acceptance of the need to intervene. This may involve breaking confidentiality. Those who have responsibility for the child should be informed unless they are suspected of the alleged abuse.

Drugs

There is no statutory obligation for schools to formulate a policy on drug education but it is likely that it will occur in connection with discipline and behaviour policies. DfEE Circular 4/95, *Drug Prevention and Schools* (DfEE 1995a), explains the law in relation to drugs. See Box 6.3.

With regard to volatile substances (for example, solvents, glues, lighter fuel, aerosol sprays, paint stripper, typewriter correction fluid and fire extinguisher fluid) the circular explains that the possession of volatile substances is not illegal. However, it is an offence in English law to supply a substance to a person aged under 18, knowing or having reasonable cause to believe that the substance or its fumes are likely to be used by that person for the purpose of causing intoxication (paragraph 68).

With reference to alcohol the circular clarifies that it is an offence to sell alcohol to anyone under the age of 18, or to give any child under the age of 5 intoxicating liquor (paragraph 75). The DfEE recommends that:

Box 6.3: The law relating to drugs

It is an offence under the Misuse of Drugs Act 1971:

- to supply or offer to supply a controlled drug* to another in contravention of the Act
- to be in possession of, or to possess with intent to supply to another, a controlled drug in contravention of the Act; it is a defence to the offence of possession that, knowing or suspecting it to be a controlled drug, the accused took possession of it for the purpose of preventing another from committing or continuing to commit an offence and that as soon as possible after taking possession of it he took all steps as were reasonably open to him to destroy the drug or deliver it in to the custody of a person lawfully entitled to take custody of it
- for the occupier or someone concerned in the management of any premises knowingly to permit or suffer on those premises the smoking of cannabis; or the production, attempted production, supply, attempted supply, or offering to supply any controlled drug (paragraph 48)

* Controlled drugs include heroin, cocaine, crack, LSD, Ecstasy, amphetamines and cannabis

---

Schools should liaise closely with their local police force to ensure that there is an agreed policy for dealing with the range of incidents which might arise involving illegal drugs ... The secretary of state would expect the police to be informed when illegal drugs are found on a pupil or on school premises. The law permits school staff to take temporary possession of a substance suspected of being a controlled drug for the purpose of protecting a pupil from harm and from committing the offence of possession. They should hand the substance to the police who will be able to identify whether it is an illegal drug and school staff should not attempt to analyse or taste an unidentified substance.

(DfEE 1995a: paragraph 49)

Paragraph 47 advises:

> Where a pupil discloses to a teacher that he or she is taking drugs the teacher should make clear to the pupil that he or she can offer no guarantee of confidentiality given the seriousness of drug misuse. A teacher might point to sources of confidential information and advice and to treatment and rehabilitation services to help those who are misusing illegal drugs to stop.

Paragraph 44 suggests: 'Consideration should be given to the provision of appropriate counselling and support within the general pastoral arrangements.' The circular also suggests schools should be aware of specialist agencies and helplines.

Criminal activity

There is no duty to disclose to the police that a child has committed a criminal offence, with the exception of threats or disclosures of criminal offences under the Prevention of Terrorism (Temporary Provisions) Act 1989. However, it is important to avoid aiding and abetting the commission of an offence. For instance, under the Misuse of Drugs Act 1971, it is illegal to allow premises to be used for the smoking of cannabis or opium or the illegal consumption and supply of controlled drugs. If a teacher is told that drugs are being passed around or sold within school and she takes no action, her inactivity could be seen as aiding and abetting. Having stated that there is no legal duty to pass on information to other agencies it is seen as a matter of good practice to pass on such information (that is, it is a moral duty). There is no hard and fast rule as to when to disclose, but government guidance encourages passing on confidential information, even if it is without the child's consent or against the child's wishes, where there is risk of significant harm without further help or intervention.

Access to records

Under the Education (School Records) Regulations 1989 (DES 1989) a pupil's parent or the pupil if over 18 has a right to access curricular records about the pupil. They may also have access to other educational records via a request to the governing body. Subject to certain exceptions young people may apply for access to their school records at the age of 16.

Under the Data Protection Act 1984, chapter 35, people are allowed access to information about themselves which is stored on computer or on back-up media. If applicants are under 18, the information will only be disclosed to them if the holder of the information believes that they understand the nature of such a request.

The Access to Personal Files Act 1987, chapter 37, allows individuals access to manual files containing information about themselves recorded since 1 April 1989. Applicants under 18 must satisfy the record holder that they understand the nature of the request they are making. Access will be refused where the authority considers that the access is likely to result in serious harm to the physical or mental health or the emotional condition of the young person, or when third parties refuse to give their consent to disclosure.

Child protection records can be kept on computer and are exempt from the disclosure provisions of the Data Protection Act 1984. For manual records, the Education (School Records) Regulations 1989 do not authorize or require the disclosure of any information on record relating to actual, alleged or suspected child abuse. If a case of alleged child abuse comes to court, the court may require the school to produce its child protection records. Child protection records should be kept securely locked (DfEE 1995b: paragraph 27).

Good practice for keeping child protection records includes noting the date, event and action taken in cases of suspected child abuse or when the child is placed on the child protection register. Paragraph 28 of the circular suggests what should be included in subsequent reports prepared for child protection conferences.

Physical contact

DfEE Circular 10/95 (DfEE 1995b) advises teachers 'to be sensitive to a child's reaction to physical contact and to act appropriately'. It also advises teachers 'not to touch pupils in ways or on parts of the body that might be considered indecent'.

Summary

Teachers need to be familiar with:

- relevant legislation
- relevant DfEE circulars
- individual school policies.

They should also have clear information about:

- resources available in school
- national and local resources
- the referral system
- record keeping
- child protection procedures
- parents' rights
- access to consultation.

Conclusion

It is important that teachers are familiar with relevant legislation and school procedures but a balance has to be struck between holding this knowledge and being able to respond sensitively to students. Great care has to be taken whenever a student makes a disclosure of abuse, intimates that she is about to disclose details of abuse, or asks for total confidentiality. In the majority of instances students' problems do not raise legal or ethical issues for the teacher but the teacher always has to keep this possibility in mind.

For a teacher to be an effective helper she needs to be able to create a safe trusting environment in which a student can feel secure enough to explore her problems. Confidentiality cannot be offered and a teacher has to work with this limitation. She may need to explain this to an individual student but in the main a good teacher can exercise her professional judgement and common sense.

* * *

Teachers have always been and will continue to be immensely significant people in young people's lives. They have the opportunity to influence young lives for the better. This is what makes working with young people so rewarding. Timely help not only meets an immediate need but often prevents a problem from becoming serious or long term. Education is not just about passing on knowledge, or creating a good environment for learning, but also about caring for the needs of the whole person. Attending to the guidelines and related issues discussed in these pages, and offering counselling and pastoral skills to students, goes some way to achieving the pursuit of a complete education.

Useful organizations and addresses

Accept Services UK
724 Fulham Road
London, SW6 5SE

Telephone: 0171 371 7555 and 0171 371 7477
National organization providing information on alcohol, tranquillizer, and drug problems.

Adfam National (The National Charity for Families of Drug Users)
Waterbridge House
32–36 Loman Street
London, SE1 0EE

Telephone: 0171 928 8900

Al-Anon/Alateen (UK and Eire)
61 Great Dover Street
London, SE1 4YF

Helpline (24 hr): 0171 403 0888
E-mail: info@Al-Anon-Alateen.org
Website: www.Al-Anon-Alateen.org

Albany Trust Counselling
280 Balham High Road
London, SW17 7AL

Telephone: 0181 767 1827
Provides counselling for sexual identity problems.

Alcohol Concern
Waterbridge House
32–36 Loman Street
London
SE1 0EE

Telephone: 0171 928 7377
E-mail: alccon@popmail.dircon.co.uk
Website: www.alcoholconcern.org.uk
Provides information on local alcohol advisory services.

Alcoholics Anonymous (AA)
PO Box 1
Stonebow House
Stonebow
York
YO1 2NJ

Telephone: 01904 644026   (UK)
                 0141 221 9027   (Scotland)
                 01232 681084   (Northern Ireland)
                 00 353 1 4538998 (Ireland)
Helpline: 0171 352 3001
Asian helpline: 0345 320202

Anti-Bullying Campaign
185 Tower Bridge Road
London
SE1 2UF

Helpline: 0171 378 1446
E-mail: anti-bullying@compuserve.com

British Association for Counselling
1 Regent Place
Rugby
Warwickshire
CV21 2VT

Telephone: 01788 550899 (Administration)
            01788 578328 (Information)
E-mail: bac@bac.co.uk
Website: www.bac.co.uk

British Dyslexia Association
98 London Road
Reading
RG1 5AU

Telephone: 0118 966 8271

British Pregnancy Advisory Service
Austy Manor
Wootton Wawen
Solihull
West Midlands
B59 6BX

Telephone: 01564 793225
Helpline: 0345 304030
E-mail: marketing@bpas.demon.co.uk

Brook Advisory Centres
165 Grays Inn Road
London
WC1X 8UD

Telephone: 0171 713 9000
Helpline (24 hr): 0171 617 8000
Website: www.brookcentres.org.uk
Provides information about sexual problems and contraception.

Campaign Against Bullying
72 Lakelands Avenue
Upper Kilmacud Road
Stillorgan
Co. Dublin
Republic of Ireland

Telephone: 00 353 1 887976

Childline
Freepost 1111
London
N1 0BR

Telephone: 0171 239 1000
Helpline (24 hr): 0800 1111
Website: www.childline.org.uk

Children's Legal Centre
University of Essex
Wivenhoe Park
Colchester
CO4 3SQ

Telephone: 01206 872466
Advice line: 01206 873820
E-mail: clc@essex.ac.uk
Concerned with the rights of children.

Citizens Advice Scotland (CAS)
26 George Square
Edinburgh
EH8 9LD

Telephone: 0131 667 0156

Commission for Racial Equality
Elliot House
Allington Street
London
SW1E 5EH

Telephone: 0171 828 7022

Compassionate Friends
53 North Street
Bristol
BS3 1EN

Telephone: 0117 966 5202
Helpline: 0117 953 9639
National self-help organization of parents whose child has died.

Cruse Bereavement Care
Cruse House
126 Sheen Road
Richmond
Surrey
TW9 1UR

Telephone: 0181 940 4818
Helpline: 0181 332 7227
Offers counselling for all bereavements.

Department of Health
Information Division
Publicity Section
5th Floor
Skipton House
80 London Road
Elephant and Castle
London, SE1 6LW

Health literature: 0800 555777
Health information: 0800 665544

Directory of Alcohol, Drug and Related Services in the Republic of Ireland
Health Promotions Unit
Department of Health
Hawkins House
Dublin 2

Telephone: 00 353 1 6714711

Divorce Mediation and Counselling Service
38 Ebury Street
London, SW1W 0LU

Telephone: 0171 730 2422

Eating Disorder Association
1st Floor
Wensum House
103 Prince of Wales Road
Norwich
Norfolk
NR1 1DW

Telephone: 01603 621414
Youth helpline: 01603 765050
E-mail: eda@netcom.co.uk
Website: www.gurney.org.uk/eda/

Family Planning Association (FPA)
2–12 Pentonville Road
London, N1 9FP

Telephone: 0171 837 5432

FFLAG (Families and Friends of Lesbians and Gays)
PO Box 153
Manchester
M60 1LP

Telephone: 0161 748 3452
Provides a befriending and counselling service and details of local
helplines.

42nd Street
2nd Floor
Swan Buildings
20 Swan Street
Manchester
M4 5JW

Helpline: 0161 832 0170
Mental health resource for 14- to 25-year-olds.

Gamblers Anonymous and Gam-Anon (GA)
PO Box 88
London
SW10 0EU

Helpline (24 hr): 0171 384 3040

Irish Society for the Prevention of Cruelty to Children (ISPCC)
20 Molesworth Street
Dublin 2
Republic of Ireland

Telephone: 00 353 1 6794944
Childline: 1-800 666 666
E-mail: ispcc@ispcc.ie
Website: www.ispcc.ie

Kidscape Campaign for Children's Safety
152 Buckingham Palace Road
London
SW1W 9TR

Telephone: 0171 730 3300
E-mail: website@kidscape.org.uk
Website: dialspace.dial.pipex.com/town/square/gaj28
Offers telephone counselling on bullying, abuse and suicide and
provides helpful literature.

Lesbian and Gay Christian Movement
Oxford House
Derbyshire Street
London
E2 6HG

Telephone: 0171 739 1249
Helpline: 0171 739 8134
E-mail: lgcm@churchnet.ucsm.ac.uk

Lesbian Youth Support Information Service (LYSIS)
PO Box 8
Todmorden
Lancashire
OL14 5TZ

Telephone: 01706 817235

London Lesbian and Gay Switchboard
PO Box 7324
London
N1 9QS

Telephone: 0171 837 6768
Helpline (24 hr): 0171 837 7324
E-mail: admin@llgs.org.uk
Website: www.llgs.org.uk

London Rape Crisis Centre (LRCC)
PO Box 69
London
WC1X 9NJ

Telephone: 0171 916 5466
Helpline (24 hr): 0171 837 1600

MIND (National Association for Mental Health)
Granta House
15–19 Broadway
London
E15 4BQ

Telephone: 0181 522 1728 and 0181 519 2122
Helpline: 0345 660163
Website: www.mind.org.uk

MIND Cymru
23 St. Mary Street
Cardiff
CF1 2AA

Telephone: 01222 395123
Helpline: 0345 660163

National AIDS Trust (NAT)
New City Cloisters
188–196 Old Street
London
EC1V 9FR

Telephone: 0171 814 6767
E-mail: info@nat.org.uk
Website: www.nat.org.uk

National Association of Citizens Advice Bureaux
115–123 Pentonville Road
London
N1 9LZ

Telephone: 0171 833 2181
Website: www.nacab.org.uk

National Council for One Parent Families (NCOPF)
255 Kentish Town Road
London
NW5 2LX

Telephone: 0171 267 1361

National Drugs Helpline
Telephone: 0800 776600 (24 hr information)

National Friend (FRIEND)
BM National Friend
London
WC1N 3XX

Telephone: 0171 837 3337
Provides information to gay, lesbian, and bisexual people.

National Newpin
Sutherland House
35 Sutherland Square
London, SE17 3EE

Telephone: 0171 703 6326
Offers support to parents and children to achieve positive changes in their relationships.

National Self Harm Network
c/o Survivors Speak Out
34 Osnaburgh Street
London, NW1 3ND

Telephone: 0171 916 5472

National Society for the Prevention of Cruelty to Children (NSPCC)
42 Curtain Road
London, EC2A 3NH

Telephone: 0171 825 2500
Helpline (24 hr): 0800 800500
E-mail: info@nspcc.org.uk

National Stepfamilies Association
Chapel House
18 Hatton Place
London, EC1N 8JH

Telephone: 0171 209 2464
Helpline: 0990 168388
E-mail: tnsa@ukonline.co.uk

Relate (National Marriage Guidance Council)
Herbert Gray College
Little Church Street
Rugby
Warwickshire
CV21 3AP

Telephone: 01788 573241
E-mail: it@national.relate.org.uk
Website: www.relate.org.uk

Release
388 Old Street
London, EC1V 9LT

Telephone: 0171 729 9904
Helpline (24 hr): 0171 603 8654
Helpline – Drugs in Schools: 0345 366666
E-mail: info@release.org.uk
Provides information and advice on drug-related problems.

Research Group on Chemical Dependency
Graham House
1–5 Albert Square
Belfast, BT1 3EQ

Telephone: 01232 240900
Provides information on drugs services in Northern Ireland.

Re-Solv
The Society for the Prevention of Solvent and Volatile Substance
Abuse
30a High Street
Stone
Staffordshire, ST15 8AW

Telephone: 01785 817885

Royal Scottish Society for the Prevention of Cruelty to Children
(RSSPCC)
Melville House
41 Polworth Terrace
Edinburgh, EH11 1NU

Telephone: 0131 337 8539

Samaritans
10 The Grove
Slough, SL1 1QP

Telephone: 01753 532713
Helpline (24 hr): 0345 909090 (UK)
Helpline (24 hr): 1850 609090 (Republic of Ireland)
E-mail: jo@samaritans.org (Sender's E-mail
address passed on)
E-mail: samaritans@anon.twwells.com (Sender's E-mail
address *not* passed on)
Website: www.samaritans.org

Scottish Drug Forum
5 Waterloo Street
Glasgow
G2 6AY

Telephone: 0141 221 1175
Provides information on drugs services in Scotland.

Shout
Bristol Crisis Service for Women
PO Box 654
Bristol
BS99 1XH

Telephone: 0117 925 1119
Offers helpline and newsletter on self-injury.

Solicitors' Family Law Association
PO Box 302
Orpington
Kent
BR6 8QX

Telephone: 01689 850227
Provides list of solicitors who promote a constructive, conciliatory
approach to divorce.

Standing Conference on Drug Abuse (SCODA)
Waterbridge House
32–36 Loman Street
London
SE1 0EE

Telephone: 0171 928 9500
E-mail: info@scoda.demon.co.uk
Provides details of local services throughout the country.

Terrence Higgins Trust
52–54 Grays Inn Road
London
WC1X 8JU

Telephone: 0171 831 0330
Helpline: 0171 242 1010
E-mail: info@tht.org.uk
Website: www.tht.org.uk
Offers information and counselling to people with HIV and Aids.

Trust for the Study of Adolescence Ltd
23 New Road
Brighton
East Sussex
BN1 1WZ

Telephone: 01273 693311
E-mail: tsa@pavilion.co.uk

Victim Support
Cranmer House
39 Brixton Road
London
SW9 6DZ

Telephone: 0171 735 9166

Welsh Drug and Alcohol Unit
4th Floor
St. David's House
Wood Street
Cardiff
CF1 1EY

Telephone: 01222 667766
Provides details of drugs services in Wales.

Women's Therapy Centre
6 Manor Gardens
London
N7 6LA

Telephone: 0171 263 7860
Helpline: 0171 263 6200

Young Carers
c/o Carers' National Association
20–25 Glasshouse Yard
London
EC1A 4JT

Telephone: 0171 490 8818
Advice line: 0345 573369
Provides information and advice to young carers.

Young Minds Trust
102–108 Clerkenwell Road
London
EC1M 5SA

Telephone: 0171 336 8445
Helpline: 0345 626376
E-mail: young.minds@ukonline.co.uk
Website: www.youngminds.org.uk
Offers information and advice on mental health of children, young people and their families.

Youth Access
1a Taylor's Yard
67 Alderbrook Road
London
SW12 8AD

Telephone: 0181 772 9900
Provides information about counselling services for young people throughout the country.

Further reading

For helplines and classified index of specialist groups see the *Voluntary Agencies Directory*, London: NCVO Publications.

Bond, T. (1993) *Standards and Ethics for Counselling in Action*. London: Sage.

British Association for Counselling (1999) *Code of Ethics and Practice Guidelines for Those Using Counselling Skills in their Work*. Rugby: BAC.

Carkhuff, R.R. (1984) *Helping and Human Relations*. Amherst, MA: Human Resource Development Press.

Carkhuff, R.R. (1993) *The Art of Helping*. Amherst, MA: Human Resource Development Press.

Children's Legal Centre (1996) *Offering Children Confidentiality: Law and Guidance*. Colchester: the Children's Legal Centre, University of Essex.

D'Ardenne, P. and Mahtani, A. (1989) *Transcultural Counselling in Action*. London: Sage.

Egan, G. (1975) *The Skilled Helper*. Monterey, CA: Brooks-Cole.

Eleftheriadou, Z. (1994) *Transcultural Counselling*. London: Central Book Publishing.

Hamblin, D. (1984) *Pastoral Care: A Training Manual*. Oxford: Blackwell.

Hamblin, D. (1993) *The Teacher and Counselling*. Hemel Hempstead: Simon & Schuster.

Ivey, A. and Authier, J. (1978) *Microcounseling*. Springfield, IL: Charles C. Thomas.

Jacobs, M. (1982) *Still Small Voice*. London: SPCK.

Jacobs, M. (1999) *Swift to Hear*. London: SPCK.

Kennedy, E. and Charles, S. (1990) *On Becoming a Counsellor*. Dublin: Gill and Macmillan.

Lago, C. and Thompson, J. (1989) *Race, Culture and Counselling*. Buckingham: Open University Press.

McLeod, J. (1998) *Introduction to Counselling*, 2nd edn. Buckingham: Open University Press.

Nelson-Jones, R. (1983) *Practical Counselling Skills*. Eastbourne: Holt Rinehart and Winston.

Pedersen, P. (1987). *Handbook of Cross Cultural Counselling and Therapy*. New York: Praeger.

Rogers, C. (1951) *Client-centered Therapy*. London: Constable.

Rogers, C. (1961) *On Becoming a Person*. London: Constable.

Skynner, R. and Cleese, J. (1983) *Families and How to Survive Them*. London: Methuen.

References

Appell, M.L. (1963) Self-understanding for the guidance counselor, *Personnel and Guidance Journal*, 42: 143–8.

Arbuckle, D.S. (1950) *Teacher Counseling*. Reading, MA: Addison-Wesley.

Arbuckle, D.S. (1965) *Counseling: Philosophy, Theory and Practice*. Boston: Allyn and Bacon.

Arbuckle, D.S. (1966) *Pupil Personnel Services in the Modern School*. Boston: Allyn and Bacon.

Argyle, M. (1983) *The Psychology of Interpersonal Behaviour*, 4th edn. London: Penguin.

BAC (British Association for Counselling) (1998) *Code of Ethics and Practice for Counsellors*. Rugby: BAC.

BAC (British Association for Counselling) (1999) *Code of Ethics and Practice Guidelines for Those Using Counselling Skills in their Work*. Rugby: BAC.

Beloff, M. and Mountfield, H. (1994) *Sex Education in Schools: A Joint Opinion*. London: Association of Teachers and Lecturers.

Berne, E. (1966) *Games People Play: The Psychology of Human Relationships*. London: Andre Deutsch.

Bolger, A.W. (1982) *Counselling in Britain*. London: Batsford Academic and Educational Limited.

Brammer, L.M. (1976) *The Helping Relationship: Process and Skills*. Englewood Cliffs, NJ: Prentice-Hall.

Brammer, L.M. and Shostrum, E.L. (1968) *The Therapeutic Psychology*. Englewood Cliffs, NJ: Prentice-Hall.

Brook Advisory Centres (1996) *What Should I Do?* London: Brook Advisory Centres.

CACE (Central Advisory Council for Education) (England) (1959) *15 to 18*, Vol.1 (*Crowther Report*). London: HMSO.

CACE (Central Advisory Council for Education) (England) (1963) *Half our Future* (*Newsom Report*). London: HMSO.

CACE (Central Advisory Council for Education) (England) (1967) *Children and their Primary Schools*, Vol.1 (*Plowden Report*). London: DES.

Cameron, N. (1963) *Personality Development and Psychopathology: A Dynamic Approach.* Boston: Houghton Mifflin.

Carkhuff, R.R. and Pierce, R.M. (1975) *Trainer's Guide: The Art of Helping.* Amherst, MA: Human Resource Development Press.

Children's Legal Centre (1996) *Offering Children Confidentiality: Law and Guidance.* Colchester: Children's Legal Centre, University of Essex.

Darwin, C. (1872) *The Expression of the Emotions in Man and Animals.* London: John Murray.

DES (Department of Education and Science) (1989) *Education (School Records) Regulations.* London: HMSO.

DfEE (Department for Education and Employment) (1994a) *Education Act 1993: Sex Education in Schools*, Circular 5/94. Sudbury: DfEE Publications Centre.

DfEE (Department for Education and Employment) (1994b) *The Education of Children with Emotional and Behavioural Difficulties*, Circular 9/94. Sudbury: DfEE Publications Centre.

DfEE (Department for Education and Employment) (1995a) *Drug Prevention and Schools*, Circular 4/95. Sudbury: DfEE Publications Centre.

DfEE (Department for Education and Employment) (1995b) *Protecting Children from Abuse: The Role of the Education Service*, Circular 10/95. Sudbury: DfEE Publications Centre.

DfEE (Department for Education and Employment) (1998) *Requirements for Courses of Initial Teacher Training*, Circular 4/98. Sudbury: DfEE Publications Centre.

DfEE (Department for Education and Employment) (1997) *School Governors: A Guide to the Law.* Sudbury: DfEE Publications Centre.

Douglas, J.W.B. (1964) *The Home and the School: A Study of Ability and Attainment in the Primary School.* London: MacGibbon and Kee.

DHSS (Department of Health and Social Security) (1988) *Report of the Inquiry into Child Abuse in Cleveland 1987* (Butler-Sloss Report). London: HMSO.

Edelwich, J. (1980) *Burn-out: Stages of Disillusionment in the Helping Professions.* New York: Human Sciences Press.

Egan, G. (1975) *The Skilled Helper.* Monterey, CA: Brooks-Cole.

Egan, G. (1986) Characteristics of classroom teachers' mentor–protégé relationships, in Gray, W. and Gray, M.M., *Mentoring: A Comprehensive Annotated Bibliography of Important References.* Vancouver, BC: International Association for Mentoring.

Ekman, P., Friesen, W. and Ellsworth, P. (1972) *Emotion in the Human Face*. Elmsford, NY: Pergamon Press.

Hall, E.T. (1977) *Beyond Culture*. Garden City, NY: Anchor Books/Doubleday.

Harper, R., Wiens, A. and Matarazzo, J. (1978) *Non Verbal Communication: The State of the Art*. New York: John Wiley.

Holden, A. (1971) *Counselling in Secondary Schools: With Special Reference to Authority and Referral*. London: Constable.

Home Office (1991) *Working Together Under the Children Act 1989: A Guide to Arrangements for Inter-agency Cooperation for the Protection of Children from Abuse*. London: HMSO.

Jacobs, M. (1999) *Swift to Hear*, 2nd edn. London: SPCK.

Jones, A. (1970) *School Counselling in Practice*. London: Ward Lock Educational.

Jones, A. (1984) *Counselling Adolescents: School and After*, 2nd edn. London: Kogan Page.

Keppers, G.L. (1956) Organizing guidance services – specialists speak, *Clearing House*, 31: 216–20.

Lang, G. and van der Molen, H. (1990) *Personal Conversations: Roles and Skills for Counsellors*. London: Routledge.

Mabey, J. and Sorensen, B. (1995) *Counselling for Young People*. Buckingham: Open University Press.

Mehrabian, A. (1971) *Silent Messages*. Belmont, CA: Wadsworth.

Musgrove, F.L.E.H. (1976) *The Family, Education and Society*. London: Routledge and Kegan Paul.

NAMH (National Association for Mental Health) (1970) *School Counselling: Report of a Working Party of the NAMH on Counselling in Schools*. London: NAMH.

Newman, B.M. and Newman, P.R. (1979) *Development through Life: A Psychosocial Approach*, revised edn. Homewood, IL: Dorsey Press.

Newson, J. and Newson, E. (1963) *Infant Care in an Urban Community*. London: Allen and Unwin.

Newson, J. and Newson, E. (1968) *Four Years Old in an Urban Community*. London: Allen and Unwin.

Noonan, E. (1983) *Counselling Young People*. London: Methuen.

Patterson, C.H. (1971) *An Introduction to Counseling in the School*. New York: Harper and Row.

Reik, T. (1948) *Listening with the Third Ear*. New York: Grove Press.

Ribbins, P. and Best, R. (1985) Pastoral care: theory, practice and the growth of research, in Lang, P. and Marland, M. (eds) *New Directions in Pastoral Care*. Oxford: Blackwell.

Richardson, J. (1979) Objections to personal counselling in schools, *British Journal of Guidance and Counselling*, 7: 129–43.

Rogers, C.R. (1951) *Client-centered Therapy*. London: Constable.

Rudduck, J., Chaplain, R. and Wallace, G. (1996) *School Improvement – What Can Pupils Tell Us?* London: David Fulton Publishers.

Skinner, B.F. (1953) *Science and Human Behaviour*. New York: Macmillan.

Truax, C.B. and Carkhuff, R.R. (1967) *Toward Effective Counseling and Psychotherapy*. New York: Aldine Publishing Company.

Tyler, L.E. (1961) *The Work of the Counselor*. New York: Appleton-Century-Crofts.

Watson, J.B. (1924) *Behaviourism*. New York: People's Institute.

Williams, K. (1973) *The School Counsellor*. London: Methuen.

Wrenn, C.G. (1962) *The Counselor in a Changing World*. Washington: American Personnel and Guidance Association.

Index

TOWARDS BULLY-FREE SCHOOLS
INTERVENTIONS IN ACTION

Derek Glover, Netta Cartwright with Denis Gleeson

This book considers the progress made towards changing pupil attitudes to bullying in twenty-five secondary schools. It begins with a consideration of the present situation and looks at the way in which policies have been developed to make school life more enjoyable for all pupils. It recognizes that families and the community at large are also involved and considers how schools can integrate their anti-bullying work with social activities, and the subject curriculum. It shows a way forward for those schools and parents who are seeking to bring about change.

Three questions are addressed:

- How can schools change attitudes so that there is a decline in all forms of bullying behaviour?
- What difference does action against bullying make to pupil life and the quality of teaching and learning?
- Is action leading to a longer term improvement in the school society?

The book is directed at those responsible for policy development in schools and colleges. It relies heavily upon case study material and so is more lively than many educational books. It will attract school governors and parents who are interested in the subject and will also be of value to those in teacher education.

Contents
Preface – Feeling of security – Me – coming to terms with self-image – Getting on with others – School culture – School policies – Reaching the parents – The community – Changing attitudes – They did it this way – Taking stock – Bibliography – Index.

192pp   0 335 19929 1 (Paperback)   0 335 19930 5 (Hardback)

COUNSELLING FOR YOUNG PEOPLE

Judith Mabey and Bernice Sorensen

This book gives a wide picture of the diversity of counselling services available to young people in Britain today, with special focus on schools and young people's counselling services. It sets these services in their historical context and describes how they have evolved. The book puts forward theoretical models for working with young clients and discusses counselling issues as they relate to work with this age group. In addition it considers some of the pitfalls counsellors may encounter in working alongside other professionals and within agencies. It includes discussion on ethical issues, non-discriminatory practice, confidentiality and child protection. The book is enlivened by case material and by examples of good practice and interesting initiatives from around the country. It will be of particular interest to counsellors, teachers, youth workers, social workers and counselling students interested in working with this age group.

Features
• Illustrated throughout with case material
• Wide discussion of ethical issues
• Examples of good practice and new initiatives
• Gives theoretical models for counselling young people

Contents
The development of counselling for young people – Counselling for young people – The practice of counselling for young people – Specific issues in counselling for young people – Professional relationships in counselling for young people – A critique of counselling for young people – Appendix – References – Index.

160pp   0 335 19298 X (paperback)

CHILD AND ADOLESCENT THERAPY: A HANDBOOK

David A. Lane and Andrew Miller (eds)

Major changes are happening in child and adolescent therapy. The contexts in which the work is done, the range of problems tackled, and the models of intervention adopted are all in flux. This book is an overview of current developments. It presents diverse practice in multiple settings; it looks at the changing agenda for therapy, and the evaluation of interventions. It explores the challenges in play therapy, with non-speaking children, for the management of trauma, in child abuse, bullying and school phobia. In terms of settings, contributors cover the residential therapeutic community, the child guidance clinic, multidisciplinary approaches to support the school, and therapy in the community. In general, it reflects the excitement (and confusions) in current child and adolescent therapy, and is an important resource for trainee and practising professionals in, for instance, social work, the health services, therapy and counselling, educational psychology and special educational needs.

Contents

Part I: The changing agenda – Child and adolescent therapy: a changing agenda – Evaluation of interventions with children and adolescents – Part II: Practice – An interactive approach to language and communication for non-speaking children – The barefoot play therapist: adapting skills for a time of need – Abuse of children – School phobia – Bullying – The management of trauma following disasters – Part III: Settings – The residential community as a therapeutic environment – The Child Guidance Clinic: problems and progress for the 1990s – School support: towards a multi-disciplinary approach – Change in natural environments: community psychology as therapy – Index.

Contributors

Nigel Blagg, Maria Callias, Phil Christie, Danya Glaser, Peter Gray, Neil Hall, Roy Howarth, David A. Lane, Monica Lanyado, Andrew Miller, Elizabeth Newson, John Newson, Jim Noakes, Wendy Prevezer, Martin Scherer, Ruth M. Williams and William Yule.

272pp   0 335 09890 8 (Paperback)   0 335 09891 6 (Hardback)